D0786894

Starting from Sleep

Starting from Sleep

NEW AND SELECTED POEMS

Charles Martin

SEWANEE WRITERS' SERIES / THE OVERLOOK PRESS

First published in the United States in 2002 by
The Overlook Press, Peter Mayer Publishers, Inc.
Woodstock & New York

WOODSTOCK:
One Overlook Drive
Woodstock, NY 12498
www.overlookpress.com
[for individual orders, bulk and special sales, contact our Woodstock office]

NEW YORK:
141 Wooster Street
New York, NY 10012

∞ The paper used in this book meets requirements for paper
permanence as described in the ANSI Z39.48-1992 standard.

Library of Congress Cataloging-in-Publication Data

Martin, Charles.
Starting from sleep : new and selected poems / Charles Martin.
p. cm. — (Sewanee writers' series)
I. Title. II. Series
PS3563.A72327 S68 2002   811'.54—dc21   2002066259

Book design and type formatting by Bernard Schleifer
Printed in the United States of America
FIRST EDITION
ISBN 1-58567-272-6
1 3 5 7 9 8 6 4 2

ACKNOWLEDGMENTS

My thanks to the editors of the following magazines, in which the new poems listed below first appeared: *The Formalist:* "Even as We Sleep"; *The Hudson Review:* "Against a Certain Kind of Ardency" and "Just a Smack at Larkin," "The Philosopher's Progress" and "How My Queer Uncle Came to Die at Last"; *The Sewanee Review:* "Dialogue of Stone and Stream" and "Seven Poems from the Latin of John Owen"; *Sewanee Theological Review:* "The Instrument" and "Necessity's Children"; *Southwest Review:* "To the Blackboard" and "On the Interpretation of Dreams"; *The Texas Review:* "Four Poems"; *Verse:* "Still Life with Pears"; *The Yale Review:* "Death Will Do Nothing." "Against a Certain Kind of Ardency" also appeared in *The Pushcart Prize 2001: XXV.*

I am thankful to the National Endowment for the Arts for a grant that aided me in working on this book, which was also supported in part by a grant from the City University of New York PSC-CUNY Research Award Program. A residency at the Ragdale Foundation is also recalled with gratitude.

The other poems printed here originally appeared (sometimes with different titles) in books edited by John T. Irwin, Robert L. Barth, and the late Harry Duncan; with gratitude I acknowledge their generous and thoughtful work on my behalf. These poems were previously published in the following magazines: *Arion:* "Tonight's Jeopardy"; *Boulevard:* "Design," "A Burial at Shanidar," "Metaphor of Grass in California," "Easter Sunday, 1985," "Stanzas after *Endgame*"; *The Chronicle:* "Making Faces"; *Cumberland Poetry Review:* "July 1914," "Mandelstam in Transit"; *The Epigrammatist:* "Souvenirs of the Late War"; *The Formalist:* "The Two of Them," "Neither Here nor There," "To a Snapping Turtle, Lately Hatched," "Reflections after a Dry Spell"; *Hellas:* "Victoria's Secret"; *The Hudson Review:* "Speech against Stone," "Fatima, 1917"; *Inquiry:* "After the Rape of the Sabine Women"; *Janus:* "Modernism: The Short Course"; *Lemniscate:* "Vain Speculations"; *Little Magazine:* "To the Living Bait"; *Nebo:* "Complaint of the Night Watchman"; *The New Criterion:* "On Yielding to Whim"; *New England Review and Bread Loaf Quarterly:* "Three Passages from Friday"; *Ontario Review:* "A Happy Ending for the Lost Children," "Landscape without History"; *Poetry:* "Four for Theodore Roethke," "Weekend," "After," parts 1, 3, and 7 of "Institutional Life," "Heroic Attitudes," "Calvus in Ruins," "Love in the City of Reflected Light," "Sharks at the New York Aquarium"; *Sewanee Theological Review:* "Reflections after a Dry Spell"; *Threepenny Review:* "Steal the Bacon," "Breaking Old Ground" (as "From the Lost and Found"); *Verse:* "At Home with Psyche and Eros"; *Wigwag:* "Getting the Miracle Wrong."

For Johanna
closest of readers

CONTENTS

I.
Starting from Sleep: New Poems

NECESSITY'S CHILDREN

"Necessity is the mother of invention."
—Old Saw

The other children of Necessity
Are utterly disheartened now, bereft
Of hopefulness since sweet Invention left,
Bravest and brightest of their family,
Who seemed to have no choice except to be
Original, persistent, shrewd, and deft;
For whom clear water sprang from the rock, cleft
By charms bespeaking her cool mastery.

"Ah, well," the others say, "she will be back,"
And armed with their conviction—for they know
How unremittingly impassable
The world, confronted by what they all lack,
Must seem to her—they say, "It will prove so:
Necessity is the mother of us all."

ON THE INTERPRETATION OF DREAMS

The dream desires to be understood,
Just as a painting wants an eye responsive
To its vision of the beautiful and good.

Then let the dreamer start from sleep to brood
On why it so resists intelligence, if
The dream desires to be understood

As thoroughly as, say, a poem would.
For the dreamer musing (now awake and pensive)
On his vision of the beautiful and good

Knows it is meaningless until construed.
But how may he learn the significance of
The dream? Desires, to be understood,

Take shape in it: those fantasies that flood
Over our sleep, so fleeting, so intensive
In their visions of the beautiful and good,

Become the figures of our speech; renewed,
Dream-images appear to be made sense of,
And dream-desires, to be understood
In our vision of the beautiful and good.

DIALOGUE OF STONE AND STREAM

Stone:

I am the figure to your ground,
The indissoluble, the knot
You part before to get around,
The lump that overcomes your wit—

Stream:

You have it wrong: you are the ground,
And I the figure: I divide
Myself and, doubling, surround
You and then press you to my bed—

Stone:

Where I resist you! Do not take
The absence of mobility
For lack of affect: in my wake
Your tumbled waters taste of me—

Stream:

Only because my chill caress
Erases you, my lips abrade
And shape your mottled surfaces
As I see fit. Therefore, abide!

Stone:

Submit, you say? I will not, ever:
Your passing would go unremarked
If my kind were to be passed over—
A stream should not be too direct.

Stream:

I was not asking you to bow;
If I could be direct I'd say
As clear as ever I knew how,
I did not mean submit, but stay—

Stone:

But stay, then! Must I always be
Dry to your wet, calm in your rage,
The stillness of your passing by,
A book left open to your page?

Stream:

And must I always seem to be
Indifferent at best to you,
A motiveless transparency,
The shallowness you see right through?

Both:

Where stone remains and water flows,
A shadow passes over: one
Who finds the emblem we comprise
A subject to reflect upon.

TO THE BLACKBOARD

Unyielding surface of preconscious mind
And childhood presence, present ever since,
Your monolithic slab still represents
Whatever I can never get behind.
Unyielding? Yes, but never unforgiving!
—Go back a bit: for thirty years and more,
I've found you waiting for me by the door
Of all the rooms in which I've earned my living,

A *tabula rasa*, whose right-angled frame
Urges inclusion while defying sprawl,
And always as a form fixed on a wall;
So in my childhood you were just the same,
The presence I could always count upon;
And though my sums were often incorrect,
My words misspelled, you never did object
To being jabbed at with a piece of bone.

Nor did we notice your indifference
To whether we remembered or forgot
The third person singular (*amat*)
Of the verb *amare* in the present tense
Indicative: *amare* meant "to love"
In the real world that floated by outside,
Its endless possibilities denied
By your mere presence: what were you thinking of?

Swans mirrored on their pond? Foals beside mare?
The lovers, who have gone inside, undressing?
Light upon darkness, darkness repossessing

The red leaves spinning dryly through the air?
—All this, a film that passed you by completely,
Leaving no mark, unlike the ones we traced
So carefully they'd never be erased,
Scratching our little hearts out on you, neatly.

As though the weightlessness of our thought
Could outlast time! Not so: those marks of ours
Were brushed off lightly, unremarked, in showers
Of dust as the erasers clapped and coughed,
Surrounding you in clouds of gilded haze;
For if (as then and now) it seemed and seems
You figured rather largely in our dreams,
We were no part of yours, back then. These days,

If sense emerges out of sign on sign
At random, when responsibility
For what goes on and off you falls on me,
I've sense enough to credit it as mine:
For you write nothing and were never heard
—Apart from that nerve-devastating shriek
You make when chalk is dragged across your cheek—
To utter phoneme, syllable, or word.

What's to be done then is all mine to do,
And likewise mine, the reward, the glory,
Since, after all, it's me telling your story
And not you telling mine; I'm happy to,
I really am, and happy in my role
As residential existentialist,
To stand before your thought-stained palimpsest
And swipe occasionally at your soul.

But you'll live on in rooms I'll leave forever,
Confronting with your reservoir of patience
The rise of provosts and the fall of nations,
Equally present to the dull, the clever,
The hopeful, the hapless, and the bored, bored, bored;
Yet even for you, deaf oracle and dumb,
Milky-eyed seer, a time will surely come
When you will have passed on to your reward:

Tell us before you leave, before the earth
Possesses you again in shards and orts,
Whether you know an answer that supports
This whethering of mine, for what it's worth:
Whether, beyond us, there is aught to wonder
At what the meaningful was meant to mean,
At what can happen to us here, between
The momentary lightning and the thunder.

THE INSTRUMENT

The instrument that we at last perfected
After so many ages of hard work,
And with solemnities and rites, directed
To question what was out there in the dark
Beyond what we were capable of seeing,
Doing as we had ordered it, addressed
By day, by night, the origin of being,
The nameless source of names unmanifest;

But that was centuries ago, and still
Interrogation, ever more abstruse,
Persists, and in the absence of response
(Some claim there was an answer given once)
Can find no purpose but in its own will,
And for its instrument, no other use.

THE WAVE

Scholars who drew on
Themselves with chalk
And scratched what they knew on
Leaves with a stalk;

Dark eyes glimpsed peering
Out of deep green
Before disappearing
Almost unseen;

Dancers adept at
Threading the turns,
Who smiled as they leapt at
A space between horns;

Wisdom and passion,
Graces and powers—
The faintest impression
Of their lives on ours.

EVEN AS WE SLEEP

Avoidance has found someone else to blame,
Obsession seeks a mantra to repeat,
And swift with *Panic*, runs across the street
In order not to have to deal with *Shame*,
Who urges *Rage* and *Folly* to come meet
Denial, going by another name;
Now unmarked cards cost *Honesty* the game,
As *Confidence* turns out to be *Deceit*,

And *Guilt* refuses to complain about
The way she's being treated by her men,
While ever-diffident *Anxiety*
Is wondering if best is not to be,
In this dark cavern between now and when,
Of whose existence he is much in doubt.

DEATH WILL DO NOTHING

Death will do nothing to advance your claim
For everything you didn't get to do:
Life and its circumstances are the same,

And when they add the scores up for the game,
You'll get no extra points for being you;
Death will do nothing to advance your claim.

Nor should it please that someone is to blame
For the false conviction or the bad review:
Life and its circumstances are the same.

You watched and waited: orders never came.
Among the unknowns, you are known as "Who?"
Death can do nothing to advance your claim.

Your cell door won't spring open? That's a shame,
It really is, my dear. And yet it's true;
Life and its circumstances are the same,

And no one is tending the eternal flame.
A needless lesson, for you always knew
Death would do nothing to advance your claim:
Life and its circumstances are the same.

AGAINST A CERTAIN KIND OF ARDENCY

1/

I know someone so ardent of the past
He finds it hard to let bygones be gone,
And says that since the present will not last,
Yesterday only can be counted on

To offer him the one true paradigm
For keeping bad enough from turning worse.
It isn't that he minds the present time,
If he could just approach it in reverse—

Yet he'd be happy to go on repeating
What has been done (as though such repetition
Were anything but wholly self-defeating),

And seems to be unbothered in the least
That he might lose the present through attrition
By yielding so much ground to the deceased.

2/

If I believed that I'd be listened to
And not accused of soiling his white banner,
I'd offer him a very different view,
Propounded in my best postmodern manner:

I'd argue that the past would be no more
Unless we made it—made, by our making,
What it could never be mistaken for:
We bring it into being by forsaking

Its ready consolations and rewards,
And thereby setting it against the new.
And so the *arrieres-and-avants-gardes*

(So like in every way except direction)
Are both mistaken about what's to do—
Though neither would have need of my correction.

3/
A long-dead Roman poet said it better
("Better" will have to do: if I say "best"
I'll lose my argument) in a verse letter
He may have meant for us, though it's addressed

To Augustus Caesar: "Who would not lament
The way we shun the new? If innovation
Had been abhorred by the Greeks to the same extent
That it is by the citizens of our nation,

There'd be no ancients for us now to read;
Where, in what trackless wasteland, would we be?
No ancients without moderns, is my creed."

With Horace, I would argue to the last
Against a certain kind of ardency;
For what, if not the present, makes the past?

LOT'S WIFE LOOKS BACK

> *But Lot's wife behind him looked back,*
> *and she became a pillar of salt.*
>
> —Genesis 19:26

I want it told correctly from the first:
I was responsible, I had been warned,
And yet, in spite of knowing what I durst
Not do, from sheer perversity I turned,
Though not to see what there was left to see,
Which by that time was a mere pile of rubble
That held no further interest for me,
But just to make unprecedented trouble
(Not all that difficult back then), lest guile
And double-dealing fall into neglect,
And disobedience go out of style.
I did it then, for *me*, in retrospect,
And not from any inadvertency
Or out of misplaced sympathy for *them:*
Those cities of the plain were much too fancy
For His Omnipotence not to condemn.
When tourists asked me why I'd turned, I'd say
I had no choice, since I was picked by Lot;
That lost its humor when Lot passed away.
My turning back *did* complicate the plot,
Though it was certainly not *my* intention
That everything I thought or felt or knew
Should be salt-cured by divine intervention—
I was allowed my little joke or two,
But silenced otherwise. Not one more word.
Ages rolled by without another word from
The nameless wife of Lot—until the Lord

Fell silent too. These days He's unheard from,
Though not unheard *of:* the fame outlasts the act
And lives on in the collective memory
Past usefulness. Now, someone with less tact
Might argue that the same is true of me,
Though as Fates go, mine seems less disagreeable,
Providing that it doesn't last forever;
I want it known that, here, for the foreseeable
Future, I plan to stay, exuding savor.

JUST A SMACK AT LARKIN

You brushed your teeth, you washed your face,
They tucked you in, your mum and dad;
They really weren't all that bad,
They weren't always on your case;

They were as good as parents got,
Back then, and did the best they knew
With such a whining shit as you;
Were they appreciated? Not!

And you, who will not take a wife
Nor raise up kiddies of your own
Can do no more than bitch and moan!
Get over it, Phil—get a life!

PAST CLOSING TIME: Eight Epigrams

I. On Epigrams

Some poets only write the ones that close
Debate off once they've made their argument;
I am occasionally fond of those,
But much prefer the kind that keeps on playing
Past closing time: after the blade's descent,
The lopped head, lifted, says, "As I was saying . . ."

II. From the Anthology

Theodorus will be tickled pink to hear
That I am dead: when Theodorus dies,
Someone, I'm sure, will learn of his demise
And a great grin will spread from ear to ear;
When *he* dies, yet another will be joyful:
If that's the case, then why is Death called "awful?"

III. Deconstructing the Zebra

"Watch out for flailing hooves," hyenas swarm,
Whose one rule is, "Dig in while it's still warm."

IV. Safe Conduct

What is more dangerous than our loves?
Nothing, the lawyers say, nothing is more.
I saw a doctor put on rubber gloves
To pick a rubber glove up from the floor.

V. To a Reviewer

The rays that journey to us from the sun
Illuminate the kneeling congregants
Of Notre Dame and also fall upon
The donkey's rump, where fleas in transport dance.

VI. The Dispassionate Shepherd Marvels at His Flock

How is it that these selfsame lambs that bleated
So awkwardly in verse so overheated
And kicked up hooves in one another's faces
Seem now as elegant as Sandro's Graces,
Arrayed for glory (or the Archive's shelves)
In sweaters that they've knitted from themselves?

VII. On the Birthday of John Coltrane

Superbly energetic fly,
Chorusing dizzily between
The glassy smoothness of the sky
And the abrasive window screen!

VIII. Prufrock Balena

In the cool depths the lissome females tarry,
Squawking of Calimari.

PETRONIUS ON VALUES

Changed circumstances may conduce
To reappraisals,
An iron key be of more use
Than gold that dazzles;

You'd trade the rags in which you're dressed
For a sable coat?
You'll find some footpad's switchblade pressed
Against your throat:

Better to grasp a splintery oar
Than a golden crown
When your treasure ship is miles from shore
And going down.

SEVEN POEMS FROM THE LATIN OF JOHN OWEN

I. Expansive Poetry

Can I express how much I cherish you
In just one line? Not possible. Take two.

II. To a Reluctant Donor

Nothing you give me, but this—I'm in your will.
—That's less than nothing, for you aren't ill!
A gift that is swiftly given doubly pleases:
My gift for you? The swiftest of fatal diseases.

III. On Epigrams

"What 'art of brevity?' It's Art diminished!"
—Yet trust me, it's not easy to be brief,
To give, from lengthy dullness, some relief—
This poem may be boring—but it's finished.

IV. Ars Amatoria

The young read Ovid for his tender art,
But what he knows of Love is no great matter,
For Nature teaches matters of the heart
Through our eyes—not through some poet's chatter.

V. On the Lives of the Saints

Merely to read of virtue is in vain?
Not if their virtue is to entertain.

VI. The Courtier's Ladder

A courtier by many small steps rises,
Yet, for a single misstep, his demise is.
    or
A courtier by many small steps rises—
Yet, for his fall, one misstep suffices.

VII. Marital Colloquy

"Cuckolds," says Pontius, "should be ducked in ponds—"
"Learn how to swim then," his Pontia responds.

STILL LIFE WITH PEARS

Hers:
She turns from it and it begins to dry,
An oilslick tightening into the fable
Of a slowly ripening mutuality:
Two pears at rest on the edge of a table.

His:
He wonders whether it could be the same
As it had been—or was that too a fiction?
He wonders whether this one has a name.
The third pear is already out of the picture.

Another's:
"He bought it from—I don't remember who.
For months he tried to find another buyer:
I told him either it goes or else I do."

Mine:
"Yes, in a dumpster! Poor bedraggled pup!
Would you mind holding it a little higher?
Don't you just love it? Is it right side up?"

THE PHILOSOPHER'S PROGRESS

1/

How wonderful! If only we could stop
Here on these verdant isles—Isles of the Blest!
And, like the Sun's immortal horses, crop
The tender stalks, undriven, unpossessed;
—But this is not for us, not ours to rest
A moment even, for it seems that we've
No sooner touched upon, barely caressed
One yielding surface when we're made to leave
For yet another. Some of us believe
That our universe had a Designer
Who moves us toward some end we can't conceive,
At ever-greater speeds—here let me linger
For just a moment underneath that arch,
Upon this bridge, before the next forced march

2/

—But no, not mine to pause, pausing's forbidden,
And whether we move on of our own accord
Or at the hest of purposes kept hidden
From us, we *do* move: motion its own reward,
Though there are others; we are rarely bored,
And not for long, with always something new
Presenting itself as not to be ignored,
One further prospect, vista, scenic view
For us to dwell upon while passing through;
Beyond the declivities, a gentle rising
For we ascend as we go forward to,
Until the path breaks up into surprising
Discontinuities, a sudden crest
That we're swept over, and we come to rest

3/

Nowhere, precisely. Neither here nor there,
With one hat on and one hat off, askew
As to one's four-in-hand and boutonniere,
And mumbling to ourselves, *how live, what do,*
Slowly begin to stir ourselves anew,
Righting as best we can the biffed and battered;
Will we succeed this time, will we come through,
We ask as though the questions really mattered:
Some deity or other will be flattered
By our prayers, but for ourselves we right
The wronged, heal the sick, collect the scattered,
Brace up the many, and at first signs of light
Return to where we start back toward the top:
How wonderful! If only we could stop.

FOUR POEMS

1. So There

So he was there and she was there as well,
By accident. (Or had it been arranged?
It would have been impossible to tell.)
They only knew that there was something changed

Between them, without knowing what. (So smart:
How could they not have known?) Space grew around them,
Not keeping them, but setting them, apart.
And by an accident arranged, they found them-

selves in whatever this might be, together,
When in themselves each found an absence shaped
(As I have heard it) very like the other;
What could they do then, really, but accept

Whatever this would be, and let time tell?
So there you were, and there I was as well.

2. Where We Are Now

Back in that time when we were very new
To one another, I thought (with delight
In fresh discoveries by day and night
And lengthy absence to be gotten through
Before we came together to undo
The work of deprivation at first sight
Once more of one another) I would write
This poem out and send it off to you;

But where the two of us are now and whether
We are there together,
I could not have said: I was like someone gazing
Into the wrong end of a telescope,
And whether passionate and playful phrasing
Might be a portent, he could only hope.

3. Yet Here We Are

When one says *tak*ing pleasure, what both mean
Is actually something in between
Taking and giving; and in the give and take
Of making love, what is it that we make,
If not the present tense of we have been?

For us, to whom much absence is routine
And laced with hours that are dure and mean,
Often there is no pleasure—just an ache
When one says, *Take*.

Yet here we are: and as the dream machine
Records for later viewing this new scene,
We are the water and the thirst we slake
As all of our senses come awake,
And both are touched and tasted, heard and seen,
When one says, *Take*.

4. Now We Are Where

Outside your window, Rage's child, Despair,
Sharpens old grudges on his rusty file,
While Happiness has put on her best smile
And set out bravely to divide the air
And sell it back to us, so much the share;
Now Interruption has begun to dial
Wrong and right numbers, at random or with guile.
It will not find us here now: we are where

Silence and stillness have set hand in hand
And mouth on mouth; here you and I lie curled
In one another, and the spinning world
Rolls back amazed, unable to unsettle
The two of us upon our lotus petal,
Until its gentle rocking wakes us, and

Slowly at first, then slowly making haste,
The sun's a golden lion in the sky
That nothing has to do with us, who try
Each other here within; shadows are traced
On stone outside, adjusted and effaced;
The sun's a ruddy lion: you and I
Ignore him as we can. The day goes by,
A day it proved impossible to waste.

DEATH AND THE FOUR-YEAR-OLD

One afternoon that summer we had been sitting on the narrow strip of lawn above the lake, watching two young men as they slowly worked their way up the beach in front of us, sweeping a metal detector over the sand before them and stopping at the occasional *ping* to probe the damp crust carefully with a kitchen knife. Sometimes they would move the sand away with their hands until they came upon something of interest—a coin perhaps, or a rusty nail—which they would carefully examine and comment upon before tossing it back or slipping it into a pocket and moving on.

The four-year-old asked me what the men were doing, and I explained that people had dropped money—quarters, nickels and dimes—which was buried now in the sand, and the men were trying to find it with their machine.

We watched them as they worked their way up past where we were, and then we stopped. They had moved on to the other end of the beach when he turned to me and asked,

"Right your father's dead?"

"Right," I said.

"Right you liked your father a lot?"

"Right again," I said.

"Right your father's buried in the ground?"

"Right," I said again.

"If I find him for you," he said, "will you give me a quarter?"

HOW MY QUEER UNCLE CAME TO DIE AT LAST

(i.m. Frederick Martin 1908–1957)

I
Dear, debonair, intemperate,
Exotic, open, ordinary,
Precariously overweight,
Self-educated *bon vivant*,
Soft, sybaritic emissary
Of Dionysus to the Bronx,
And slyly uninhibited
Life of the party, Uncle Fred—

Dropped by a massive heart attack
Quite plausibly, the truth to tell,
One afternoon on his way back
From a late lunch at Child's or Schrafft's:
As he lay dying where he fell,
His large ironic spirit passed
Through gawkers gathered at curbside
And hailed a cab for his last ride . . .

I'd seen your death certificate,
Signed by the famous coroner:
Who would have ever questioned it?
—Surely not anyone aware
Of your strong predilection for
The good life, served up bloody rare
Along with bottomless cocktails
And your unfiltered "coffin nails."

It was the good life did you in,
As I assumed—the appetite
Whose cheerful servant you had been
Until the good life cut yours short
One winter afternoon. That night
I listened to the wind's report
And hid myself away and cried.
I learned of dying when you died.

Other lessons were more subtle,
Were even open to debate;
This one alone brooked no rebuttal,
As though some mindless hand erased
The chalked-on figures from a slate,
And all the lines a lifetime traced
Were altogether swept away
Late on one lightless winter day . . .

II
My legacy from Uncle Fred?
The bookish boy whose vision you
Sought to correct inherited
Some books of yours (which some years later
Helped to explain a thing or two)
By Oscar Wilde and Walter Pater,
And two bronze candlesticks with *putti*—
A pair, in truth, of no great beauty,

But emblematic, I still knew,
Of what were called "the finer things—"
Though what *these* were, I had no clue.

Your angels now present themselves
In memory to try their wings,
Fly to forgotten kitchen shelves
And point out what I'd long misplaced,
The hidden origins of taste

In every bottle, tin, or jar:
Wild berries crushed to silken jam,
The bright black beads of caviar,
Rock lobster tails, imported beer,
Asparagus and Smithfield ham,
So unfamiliar and so dear!
Even a can—can it be so?
Quite plainly labeled *ESCARGOTS*.

Then, as you evenly divided
Delicacies unknown before,
Even the youngest was provided
With a small portion of his own—
A kindness he's still grateful for,
Who sees a line distinctly drawn
From diverse canapés and *torten*
Through Eliot to later Auden.

III
Those afternoons of cakes and laughter
Faded to evenings that ended
With your invariant departure
For downtown and for company
More worldly-wise than that provided
By your provincial family;
Although I kept my nose in books,
I caught the grown-ups' knowing looks.

No matter what their glances meant,
Their explanations gave you cover;
The Interfaith Impediment
To me, at least, seemed plausible:
Your fiancée (*not* your lover)
Was a Jewish or a Catholic girl
Whose parents would not let her wed
A Protestant—our Uncle Fred.

Your long engagement having failed,
You bore with equanimity
Whatever grief its loss entailed.
That was a fiction through and through,
I realize: it had to be;
Back then I thought that it was true,
And even now want in some sense
For it to be not *just* pretense—

I break off and an upraised brow
Furrows my own: *"What's that you said?"*
I'm really not sure that *I* know,
But *you* must—*you're* the analyst.
"His nephew wanted Uncle Fred
Straight with an unacknowledged twist,
To be spared the humiliation
Of queerdom by association."

A liberal for my whole life,
I'm more than willing to believe
The very worst about myself:
Was I so timid that I'd wanted
A likely fiction to deceive

The childhood friends who would have taunted?
Of course—but that scenario
Assumes I would have had to know,

Which wasn't very likely, was it?
He died. The years went by. I guessed
What had been hidden in his closet,
The knowledge I had come so near,
The truth that could not be expressed.
It was his death that I thought queer.
I use the word in its old sense.
I think he died of the pretense.

IV
His death, recounted, soon assumed
Sufficient plausibility;
We mourned and our lives resumed.
And yet it left a residue
Behind—a need for secrecy,
The knot a child tries to undo
By tugging at—this doesn't work:
The knot just tightens with each jerk.

Familiar silence, a white noise
Made up of what cannot be said,
Affirming all that it denies;
In its refusal, volumes speak,
Are eloquent, could they be read:
To this young scholar, they were Greek,
Unfathomable on their shelves.
My life went on. It tried on selves,

Adjusting them until they fit
My aptitudes or sense of style,
And on those days I thought of it,
His death became one reason why
I ought to jog that extra mile
Or give up (on the umpteenth try)
The weed that killed him, as I thought.
Silence would seem to have won out,

Until, when almost all who knew
The secret were themselves deceased,
It was at last my mother who
One afternoon abruptly said,
"It wasn't cardiac arrest—
Somebody killed your Uncle Fred,
Beat him to death so brutally
That when your father claimed him, he

Could only recognize him by
The bloodstained clothing that he wore—
The coroner agreed to lie."
To lie? Because he had been killed?
But who killed Freddie? Where? What for?
Some questions answered, others stilled
By her final revelation:
"The men's room at Grand Central Station."

V
The first scene had to be revised:
No longer dying instantly
But torturously brutalized,
You fade out slowly, underneath

Accumulating agony
Which only ends with your last breath.
I am unable to repair
That treachery or your despair;

The brother who collapsed and died,
The other who continued, grieving;
Justice, which you have been denied,
And silence, by which you were blamed;
The years that passed with me believing
In lies of which I am ashamed;
The savagery that still deprives:
Your absence from my children's lives,

Your troubled presence in my own,
Encumbering me with the ghost
Of someone inchoately known.
I light one of your candlesticks
(The other one has gotten lost)
And watch intently as the wax
Pools steadily beneath the flame
Then overflows its shallow dam

To run in rivulets upon
The figure of Angelic Youth
Whose bronze features seem to frown
In anger—or is he just bored?
"He was no beauty, in all truth,
But still the best I could afford;
The friendless nightmare of my death
Can never be set right, and yet

Within your life, I still persist,
An influence that you call good
And find few reasons to resist,
And many to be grateful for;
Alive, I would feel gratitude
Myself, with nothing to deplore,
Nothing to alter or amend,
As I felt even at the end;

But even as a welcome guest
Within the swiftly moving lives
Of those who knew and loved me best
I am now changed past recognition,
A figure that somehow survives
The boundaries of its condition,
A fiction that your words renew;
Now let me go, and you go too."

II.
from WHAT THE DARKNESS PROPOSES

FOR A CHILD OF SEVEN,
TAKEN BY THE JESUITS

The little criminal is seized and shaken
Like a globe of snow; locked in a place without
Light or supper, he'd rather have been taken
By the red Indians he's read about
In Classic Comic Books; there the precocious
Seven-year-old absorbed atrocities
Of line and color scarcely less atrocious
Than the events themselves: Alice on her knees
In the glum forest, facing death or worse
From Magua, empurpled in his rage,
While those who love her ignorantly traverse
The awkward contours of a far-off page
Through thick and thin, through smudgy and grotesque:
A tightly rolled-up scroll on Father's desk.

BREAKING OLD GROUND

1/

What was it that roughed up and threw away
The children's toy, this plastic dinosaur
I found early this morning, where it lay
Forgotten in the muck of my backyard,
Still half-embedded in the oozy clay?
Softening winter left it stunned: it tottered
Awkwardly, until I got it to stand
On the palm and fingers of my upturned hand.

2/

Whatever took it took it by surprise,
With feline cunning or a childish shriek,
Before it could transform its painted eyes
And its impersonally molded beak
Into an aspect that would terrorize:
This one would not have turned the other cheek.
Yet here I found it in the slush, still grinning
At what had taken it and sent it spinning.

3/

Thinlidded eyes and sharply pointed teeth
Made a face equal to the ironies
That oversaw the lizard's coming forth,
Its form emerging out of molten ice
After some power deep within the earth
Had fluttered those lids, tickled those ivories,
And heaved the frost that managed the displacement
Of this emissary from the basement—

4/

Or had that grin begun to find its shape
While the poor relations all were losing theirs
In transformations they could not escape?
Over the next few hundred million years
They oozed into oil, drop by viscous drop,
Until one morning suddenly appears
An obliging lump, battered but unsubdued
After one last refinement of the crude.

5/

A raspberry fanfare, then, a serpent's hiss
To welcome this appealing, well-cast spell,
This much-diminished metamorphosis
Of the great futilities that rose and fell
So many ages ago! Perhaps I'll miss
Its soiled acrylic presence (How can I tell?)
When I put it back where it was found and leave,
Ignoring the urgent tugging at my sleeve;

6/

Why should we feel obliged to, when we find
Something we haven't lost and have no need for?
Is it our desire for the ties that bind,
However loosely knotted? Or does *it* plead for
Recognition, acceptance—was it designed
To have its own designs on us? Indeed, for
It really seems to care (Though how can it say?)
Whether it's pocketed or thrown away,

7/

It really seems to want to be our friend,
Returning, is it, out of sympathy
Or just to see how everything will end?
Waiting, in either case, for one like me
To show up some morning at the backyard fence,
A perfect stranger: who may or may not be
Impressed with what it was or where it's been,
But, taken with or by it, takes it in.

VICTORIA'S SECRET

Victorian mothers instructed their daughters, ahem,
That whenever their husbands were getting it off on them,
The only thing for it was just to lie perfectly flat
And try to imagine themselves out buying a new hat;
So, night after night, expeditions grimly set off,
Each leaving a corpse in its wake to service the toff
With the whiskers and whiskey, the lecherous ogre bent
Over her, thrashing and thrusting until he was spent.
Or so we imagine, persuaded that our forebears
Could never have had minds as unbuttoned as ours,
As our descendents will shun the kinds of repression
They think we were prone to—if thinking come back into fashion.
And here is *Victoria's Secret*, which fondly supposes
That the young women depicted in various poses
Of complaisant negligence somehow or other reveal
More than we see of them: we're intended to feel
That this isn't simply a matter of sheer lingerie,
But rather the baring of something long hidden away
Behind an outmoded conception of rectitude:
Liberation appears to us, not entirely nude,
In the form of a fullbreasted nymph, implausibly slim,
Airbrushed at each conjunction of torso and limb,
Who looks up from the page with large and curious eyes
That never close: and in their depths lie frozen
The wordless dreams shared by all merchandise,
Even the hats that wait in the dark to be chosen.

TONIGHT'S JEOPARDY

*"This ancient author is said to have died when
an eagle dropped a tortoise on his head."*
      "Who was . . . John Milton?"

That question, wildly ricocheting, travels
Throughout the empyrean's upper levels
Before it knocks a tortoise off the shelf
Where it had once paused to collect itself;

It now commences free fall—has it found
The head that it will rhyme with on the ground?
Not yet, not yet: contestant number two,
A young mother of four from Kalamazoo,

Draws hope and sustenance and from thin air
A link between the tortoise and a hare
That does not hold: *"Who was . . . Aesop?" "No . . ."*
We're left hanging for a moment or so

(Contestant number three is out to lunch
And will not try his luck or play a hunch),
While answer seeks the question still to come
And tortoise drops toward an unwitting dome

Fringed with white hair, an inexpressive mask
Weathered by questions we no longer ask,
A name our three contestants fail to guess:
"Who was the tragic poet Aeschylus?"

SOUVENIRS OF THE LATE WAR

Now stand at ease where they (and we) once quivered
Anticipating payloads undelivered:
Erect, invisible, and still awaiting
The end of our passionate debating.

A NIGHT AT THE OPERA

Flamboyant at the end,
She has her sister send
For Aeneas once more—
One last time, before
She turns away from the wall
To give the death scene all
She has, her sullen passion
Become a sharp weapon.
Spare, merciless, and quick,
That self-hating rhetoric
Lifts the flesh from her bones
And partially atones
For some of her past folly.
That Queen, that poor duped dolly,
Stripped now of all but her
Speech, rises to the pure
Outrage of poetry,
Triumphant, even as he
Flees, who will never return,
Whom she cannot hope to burn
In the fiery crucible
Of her chastened will.
And having had her say,
She torches her life away:
Flame quivers at her lips.

On one of the adamant ships
Already lost to sight,
He thinks ahead: tonight
He will not have a woman.

Already a good Roman,
Thoroughly sick of the sea,
He thinks of how easily
The strongest walls are shaken,
How cities may be taken
By cleverness or force.
Recalling the Wooden Horse
And the breech made in the wall,
He says, to no one at all,
"No fundament of stone
Is safe to build upon;
My city will be made
Of Law, my laws obeyed;
In my earth-wracking city
Will be no room for pity
Or weakness of any kind;
Strict Justice, who is blind,
And angry Mars will keep
My city while I rule,
And after, when I sleep—
A thousand years or more,
Two thousand years before . . ."

Her ardent embers cool.

GETTING THE MIRACLE WRONG

The stale, essential snowflake which was said
To be Christ's body, our Wonder Bread,
Stuck and then melted on my outthrust tongue—
That seemed a miracle. When I was young,
It happened every time I went to Mass,
And, as the priest explained it to our class,
Displaying an unconsecrated crumb
Between his right-hand forefinger and thumb,
Was something only Catholics could savor.
I found the substance wholly without flavor.

FLYING HEADS

Lopped off, they jetted wings at shoulder level
A moment after their brief lives were ended;
Skittering from the clutches of the Devil,
The little ones ascended

In formation to surround Our Savior
And fan the victors of the Church Triumphant.
Cited on the field for good behavior,
Each newly halo'd infant

Fusses and fidgets, waiting for the Day
Of Judgement, when the dead will all be sifted,
And those who've been naughty will be led away
While the righteous are uplifted.

Artists would afterward enjoy devising
Improvements on that model—if a second
Pair of wings would aid in stabilizing
Erratic flybabies, they reckoned

That a third pair would be even better:
Two wings prone, two supine, two akimbo,
According to the spirit or the letter
Of the law in Limbo,

Where some had been consigned by their Creator.
In Limbo is Latin, meaning *on the border:*
There, tiny passengers whose elevator
Has gone out of order

Wait between floors now on their way to heaven:
Some pressing noses against the emergency button,
Some hanging upside down like bats in a cavern—
Not remembered, not forgotten.

REFLECTIONS AFTER A DRY SPELL

For Howard Nemerov

"A good poet is someone who manages,
in a lifetime of standing out in thunderstorms,
to be struck by lightning five or six times."
                    —Randall Jarrell

And the one who took this literally
Is the one that you still sometimes see
In the park, running from tree to tree

On likely days, out to stand under
The right one *this* time—until the thunder
Rebukes him for yet another blunder . . .

But the one who knew it was nothing more
(That flash of lightning) than a metaphor,
And said as much, as he went out the door—

Of that one, if you're lucky, you just may find
The unzapped verse or two he left behind
On the confusion between World and Mind.

MODERNISM: THE SHORT COURSE

1/

In the beginning, it was a thin wedge that divided
    Us all along the fault line of approval,
So that we either gave our assent and applauded,
    Or else wrote letters demanding its removal.

2/

The young defended it in practice and in theory
    (In theory the more important of the two)
Until they themselves were ancient celebrities, weary
    Of having always to look back at the new.

3/

It had but one aim: to baffle all expectations
    And do whatever it intended to:
When you agreed with it, it snorted with impatience,
    And when you despised it, it agreed with you.

4/

And we, in its wake, cling to whatever keeps us afloat,
    Diminished by our having missed it, though
Man Ray's a consolation: "They say that I missed the boat,
    But all of the boats I missed sank years ago."

AT HOME WITH PSYCHE AND EROS

Not much of a reader or writer
Himself, but always hot for a good fable,
Eros has heaped the tabloids that he bought her
On Psyche's coffee table:
The HOUSEWIFE who is TAKEN UP IN RAPTURE
Rubs elbows with the ALIENS that CAPTURE
BIGFOOT'S PREGNANT DAUGHTER!

Having accepted her lover
And his limitations, Psyche still wonders
Whether a book *can't* be judged by its cover,
As on her chaise she ponders
The glossy pages of *Panache* or *Flic*
Till "Beuys at MOMA: A Feminist Critique"
Glazes her eyes over.

VAIN SPECULATIONS

What then if Ri vaThurrison had missed
When Grozmal, leaping from his brettathurk,
Uncoiled the brindled hydra with a smirk
And fell upon him? Fetid was the mist
That bleared Ri's sight, green tendrils clasped his wrist—
In one sure motion he unsheathed his dirk
And thrust it home! "My gift has done its work,"
The ancient Hag of Lower Lochmar hissed;

And as Ri stared, her wrinkles fell away
Until his eyes drank in sweet Delia's face!
They mounted Grozmal's 'thurk, and none can say
Where they rode off to, for they left no trace.
But had he missed I'm certain that today
The world would be a very different place.

TO A SNAPPING TURTLE,
LATELY HATCHED

By interrupting your mild gallop
And lifting you, a meager dollop
Of flesh resembling a scallop
                Encrusted with dirt,
I no doubt saved you from a wallop
                That would have hurt;

Eyeball to eyeball now, you blink
And faster than thought (you cannot think)
Reflexively begin to shrink
                Down to a center
Guarded by armor without a chink,
                That naught may enter.

But *one* cannot go into zero:
With too much flesh to disappear, you
Have no choice but play the hero,
                Which you do with grace,
Head jutting out, then limbs—an aero-
                naut, treading space!

So profoundly self-sufficient,
You do not even seem to want
A turtle or an elephant
                To stand upon—
No cosmological event
                Holds your attention.

You are perfection of a kind
But cannot know (you would not mind)
How utterly you're left behind.
                    Taking your side,
I put you down before the pond
                    Where you'll reside,

Your destiny, to lie in mud
(And our far more toxic crud)
With your jaws parted to the flood,
                    Wiggling your tongue
Until some darter nips its bud
                    And the trap is sprung;

Or venturing among the shallows
For waterfowl in water-willows,
Gulping a drumstick in two swallows,
                    So great your greed.
You will not boast among your fellows
                    Of my good deed,

But someday on the shore, I'll watch
A line of geese (now out of reach)
Sing your powers of retention, each
                    With one leg missing;
And what they've learned from you, they'll teach,
                    Volubly hissing.

STANZAS AFTER *ENDGAME*

1/

Hurrying toward a tiny Off-Off-Off-
Off-Broadway theater, we nimbly circumvent
An uprising, a shouting match of gruff
    Old men, untidy, indigent,
  Who find, this Sunday afternoon, a small
Stage to enact their outrage on, a transient
    Refuge from the wrecker's ball;

2/

Here artists and their lofts survive by grace
Of our needy city's celebrated
Developers, whose greed for office space
    Seems for now to have abated;
  And here men wait with rags and dirty water
To smear new grime on windshields of intimidated
    Drivers who curse, but give a quarter;

3/

Quarters accumulated buy a quart
Of *Gold Coin Extra* or *Lone Star Malt Brew*;
Others do crack or heroin, or snort
    Fumes out of bags of plastic glue;
  In the urinous storefronts where they meet,
Nodding acquaintances impatiently renew
    The ties that bind them to the street.

4/

No better place than this to stage a play
That illustrates the way the world will end,
For who will come to see it anyway,
    But the subscribers, who attend
Everything? Yet look: there, against the curb, an
Ark! Another! Whence in disbelief descend
    Voyagers—dazed, droll, suburban!

5/

Two *Short Line* buses with the audience:
The first is full of high-school kids and teachers,
The second carries senior citizens
    Clutching discount ticket vouchers;
As they negotiate front stairs and aisle,
Purplespiked mutants grimly stalk the blue-rinsed grouches
    Up and into the theater, while

6/

We in the middle find our seats and pray,
Unhopefully, that Beckett's spare precision
Survive all cries of "What did he just say?"
    And adolescent snorts of derision:
The young with their tongues in one another's ears,
And their elders talking back to television,
    Except this isn't television, dears.

7/

The lights go down and we become aware
Of someone on stage, motionless at first,
Beginning to move around a covered chair;

The way taken is at once reversed:
   Upstage, downstage, dithering left and right,
Until the tiny stage is thoroughly traversed:
     No other characters in sight.

8/
A promising beginning this is not.
From a few rows back comes an angry hiss:
"Isn't it . . . doesn't it . . . hasn't it . . . got a plot?"
     An answer started from across
The aisle is throttled down in someone's throat as
We lean into a vortex of expanding loss,
     That's taken us before we notice;

9/
New characters emerge, the sum of their
Seemingly irreversible reverses:
Hamm (underneath the covers on the chair)
     Joins *Clov* (on stage) and fiercely curses
Progenitor and Genetrix (the droll
Nagg, the winsome *Nell*) then brokenly rehearses
     Life at ground zero of the soul,

10/
Where first there is not enough and then there's more
And more of not enough, insufficiency
In slow addition, grain upon grain before
     It happens ever so suddenly
That insufficiency becomes too much
To bear, absent the hope that there might ever be
     Enough insufficiency, as such.

11/

Once there was something other than what's here,
Which is to say, a time that wasn't now:
Once shape and shapeless played with far and near,
    Brightness and shadow, fastness and flow;
Once there were places variously green
And pools they had, of clear water, wherein we saw
    Ourselves and our selves were seen—

12/

Reflections and expansions of the self!
The past not merely an accumulation!
Progressive toys on every kiddie's shelf!
    But why must we go on and on
About the something more than not enough?
No reason: even as insufficiency, redun-
    dancy, though made of sterner stuff,

13/

Is certainly as equally absurd,
Meaningless, purposeless—yet we attend,
Hang, it is fair to say, on every word
    That brings us nearer to the end
Of stillness and silence. A brief tableau,
Then darkness separates those who must stay behind
    From those who are now free to go.

14/

From this immersion we emerge subdued
And seem more careful of one another;
The elders less cranky and the young not rude

But helpful as we leave together,
    Guiding an elbow, retrieving a dropped cane
For someone old enough to be Adam's grandfather,
        And whom we'll never meet again.

15/
    Why are we so changed? Perhaps it's simple:
    A parable of Kafka's comes to mind,
    Of the leopards who break into the temple
        And drink the spirits that they find
    In consecrated vessels; their continual
Thefts (being now predictable) are soon assigned
        A part within the ritual.

16/
    Meaning emerges out of random act
    And lasts as long as there are those intent
    On finding it and keeping it intact
        In fables of the impermanent.
    We leave the theater as though illustrating
How hard that is to do. The going audience
        Begins to board the buses waiting

17/
    At curbside to recall them from this dream
    Into their lives: the young are making dates,
    Their elders trying to remember them.
        Slowly, slowly, it separates!
    Some are still standing outside the theater,
While others take off briskly down the darkening streets
        Wrapped up in their own thought, or

18/
Arguing, like these four on the corner,
About the meaning of it all, before
They set out to find themselves some dinner
    At the newly redecorated Hunan Court,
Where many fragrant wonders are provided
Soon for the delectation of one carnivore,
    Two vegetarians, one undecided.

THE PHILOSOPHER'S BALLOON

Whether the Laws that govern us were fashioned
For our benefit (who otherwise
Might find ourselves in the breathless stratosphere)
Or were meant to keep us from our rightful station
Remains unsettled, open to surmise—
But that there are Laws is absolutely clear.
We may derive the existence of these Laws
Not from the necessity of a First Cause,
Some Creator inflating us until we squeal,
But from the strings to which we are attached,
Which represent the Laws and those who make them;
That the strings attached to us are really real,
And not, as some say, just a figure of speech,
Becomes apparent only when we break them.

III.
SEQUENCE IN CALIFORNIA

ON YIELDING TO WHIM

For D.G.—someone
raised in a landscape short of rain

Someone imagines that he sees a cat
Crouching in these hot hills—another burns
For the lounging odalisk which he discerns
Couched in the same dun-colored folds of what
Is, underneath, mere stone—despite its range
Of attitudes, characters, reveries.
Two of the nearer hills, encouraged, rise
Slowly and languorously stretching change

Into a form made of the appetite
To find a form there, let the mind's eye trace
Imaginary lines to metaphor—
A cat? A woman? A moment and no more:
Mirages ordinary to a place
Stingy with water, generous with light.

METAPHOR OF GRASS IN CALIFORNIA

The seeds of certain grasses that once grew
Over the graves of those who fell at Troy
Were brought to California in the hooves
Of Spanish cattle. Trodden into the soil,

They liked it well enough to germinate,
Awakening into another scene
Of conquest: blade fell upon flashing blade
Until the native grasses fled the field,

And the native flowers bowed to their dominion.
Small clumps of them fought on as they retreated
Toward isolated ledges of serpentine,
Repellent to their conquerors.
                              In defeat,

They were like men who see their city taken,
And think of grass—how soon it will conceal
All of the scattered bodies of the slain;
As such men fall, these fell, but silently.

THE TWO OF THEM

But no, it isn't over for them yet:
They sit off by themselves, watching the sun set
    Behind the hills striated now with fog.
Two coffees, one forbidden cigarette:

They pass at intervals its glowing coal
From each to other. Pressed sheets of fog roll
    Into the valley right before a range
Of hills like mountains in a Chinese scroll,

Where fog is something dreamt of by the ocean
Beyond, a post-impressionist's impression
    Of large and little waves all pressing shoreward,
And quietly dispersing in slow motion

A few last smudgy bits of broken light:
The distant range had kept this out of sight.
    Seeing beyond it was beyond them both
Who saw no further than the coming night,

The room that would be there as certainly
As was the ocean which they could not see;
    And in that room, all they would first remember
And afterward imagine, when memory

Would no more lift a fingertip to trace
Out of the darkness, contours of a face
    Or gestures that imperceptibly once led
Into the fierce constrictions of embrace:

Persistence of the gestures that renew
Desire is the legend woven through
    Those days and nights, now to be read only
Here in what I have written of these two,

Who sit where I have put them and think about
The way it goes from certainty to doubt
    And back again until the coffee's cold
And the glowing coal is carefully stubbed out.

They leave tomorrow, taking what is theirs.
A sky magnificently shot with stars
    Has been arranged tonight to bring them in
As the last slip of sunlight disappears

Beyond the hills; and while coyotes howl
Their heartsick threnodies, a Great Horned Owl
    Gives answers to the questions that she poses
And then soars into darkness on the prowl.

A WALK IN THE HILLS
ABOVE THE ARTISTS' HOUSE

I. Neither Here nor There

Late afternoon: in studios
Where work is done or unbegun,
Disoriented poets close
The books on rough draft or revision;
Outside, as a declining sun
Takes aim at the Pacific Ocean,
A little clearing slowly fills
With those who'd like to walk the hills

Above the temporary quarters
(Emptying out now for the hike)
Where composers, artists, writers
Have settled in to make their mark,
Each different but all alike
In having gotten time to work
As much or little as we please,
And walk sometime among the trees—

Perhaps the same trees I flew over
After I managed to exchange
My sweaty feedbag for the clover
Of a few weeks' idleness;
Significant others find it strange,
But work that any artist does
Paradoxically depends
On leisure to achieve its ends.

A week ago, in some suspense,
I'd driven up a golden coast
Past signs that threatened ARMED RESPONSE,
Straining my rent-a-wreck until—
Have I gone past it? Am I lost?
A grand museum on a hill
Presented itself: with the view
I caught a glimpse of *déjà vu:*

My eyes if not my legs had been
(How did I know it?) here before:
A gate, a guard who let me in
To find the underground garage:
An elevator rose one floor
And opened up on a mirage;
I knew the place—and stood amazed
At the great villa Piso raised!

Piso, the Getty of his time
(Both men had made it big in oil),
Who built at Herculaneum
A summer refuge from the dreary
Round of urban stress and toil,
His Villa dei Papiri!
The name applied to it much later
By an Italian excavator,

Who found the room where Philodemus,
Philosopher in minor key,
Elaborated his great theme

In essay and in epigram;
Praised the mysterious faculty
For which he had no proper name:
Imagination, understood
As any art's supremest good.

Vesuvius cried, "Hold that thought!"
And all his wit and eloquence,
Unread, unheard of, lay unsought;
Oblivion's new underground
Poet and scholar in residence
(Alas!) was nowhere to be found,
Until a pickaxe let in light
On notions long kept out of sight:

Leaves of his Book, reduced to ash
And shoveled from a cluttered shelf,
Were almost thrown out with the trash:
"Oh—were those *scrolls?*" Now blackened lace.
At first uncertain of itself,
Each inkstained fragment finds a place;
There are few guides for the perplexed
When charred briquets become a text,

And text becomes a voice that lifts
Off from its backing to present
Us with long-unaccustomed gifts;
Here Philodemus criticizes
Artists who merely represent,
Then asks a question that surprises:
"Why can't a painter paint instead
A man with, say, a horse's head?

"Why can't he show us, if he wishes,
A human face upon a creature
With a tail just like a fish's?
Why must an artist be confined
To drawing images from nature,
Ignoring those that spring from mind?"
So, in a cell provided him
By Piso's will or Piso's whim,

The poet artfully composed
In well-funded isolation;
Who did not own himself, proposed
The right of artists to create,
Each from his own imagination,
Rather than merely imitate;
"For, as we grasp in our dreams,
The world is hardly what it seems.

"As our poets all inform us,
In poetry false may be true,
Great may be small, and small, enormous;
The fabulous is natural:
Cyclops complaining of the view
And Venus on her scallop shell
May have originated in a
Cheese that Piso served at dinner.

Poets had little, Piso, plenty;
He loved the prestige that accrued
To him among the cognoscenti
Who fattened on his patronage;

How could his mansion *not* include
A room for his residing sage?
As well as one for pinky rings
And for the girlfriends' slinky things.

The villa Piso built was soon
Unfit for *any* occupant;
It disappeared one afternoon
Under a flow of laval silt
That hardened into adamant.
I walked through one that had been built
In imitation of its plan
By a wealthy Californian,

Then drove to the artists' colony
Much farther north—the inspiration
Of a modern mage whose alchemy
Resulted in "la pilule d'or,"
Which helped free sex from generation,
And made a large nonprofit for
The foundation on whose real estate
I am ensconced now to create.

And where, last night, we met our host,
Who did his best to break the ice
Between the salad and the roast:
"It seems to me the life you chose
Is a continual sacrifice
That you've accepted; yet, suppose
The work you did could find no venue—
Would you be willing to continue

"If you could have no hope of any
Response from anyone at all,
Have neither fame nor love nor money,
Nor yet the thumbscrew nor the rack,
And—this, I think, would most appall-
Even indifference held back;
Given a worst-case scenario
Out of Beckett, Kafka, Poe—

"Immured in some grim *oubliette*
Whence word of you would never issue,
And none there were who would regret
Your absence from the banquet table,
Or call you up to say, 'We miss you!'
Is it—I mean would you be able,
Could you create, without the sense
Your work had use or consequence?"

Good question. Once a poet-friend
Told me that if he ever heard
The world was coming to an end—
The missile launched with his name on it—
He'd try to put in a last word
Or two on an unfinished sonnet.
Although I think that I would try to
Find someone to say good-bye to,

It is a personal decision
As to whether, at closing time,
The life or work most wants revision—
I can't do other than admire

His quest for one last, perfect rhyme,
Such a fierce refining fire—
I guess I ought to make it clear
I mean the poet's fire, here—

But if our writing matters, what
Makes it matter matters more
Than *it* does—what goes on without,
In inexpressively tremendous
Regions of after and before
And happening right now, beyond us—
All that we simply do not get:
It promises us nothing, yet

My poet-friend would have in mind
A saving grace to end up with
As I would too—I'd hope to find
An image suitably oblique:
The unilluminated moth
That fluttered from an opened book
And struggles to ascend on air
Will soon be neither here nor there.

II. Letter from Here for Now

You ask me to describe the way
I live out here—is there a routine
That I've established for my stay,
And do I have a cell or suite,
Who are the others on the scene,
And the cooking—is it fit to eat?
Important questions, which one guest will
Try to answer in this epistle.

I'll start at the alarming break
Of day, when I am least productive:
Some of us slowly come awake,
While others leap and prance like goats;
The difference can be instructive
If you're alert and taking notes,
Which I am usually not.
I take a shower (very hot),

Then amble to the kitchen, where
A neighbor infinitely kind
Is just beginning to prepare
A breakfast for however many
Rise to its bait. "Charles, look behind
Those cans and see if we've got any
More Bisquick left." The mix is found,
And obdurate dark beans are ground

Into a silt that, drop by drop,
First holds its liquor, then releases
A brew that makes the spoon stand up;
And, as my neighbor briskly stirs
Three kinds of freshly grated cheeses
With funghi, peahen eggs, and herbs
Snipped from a teeming window box,
I slice bagels and shave the lox

Into such sheer transparencies
As an optician might well use
For rosy-colored eyeglass lenses:
A salt-and-salmon-flavored tint.

Some minor touches and we're through;
Sliced oranges are dressed with mint,
The table with a fresh bouquet
Of wildflowers. What's that you say?

"This man is mad, or else a liar!"
Well, my description represents
The breakfast to which I aspire,
Our dailiness idealized—
As anyone with any sense
Would long ago have realized.
Some days *are* special—but on most
Others it's cereal or toast,

A cup of coffee, then a second
Which I take back into my study.
By now I've pretty much awakened,
I'm sitting at my writing table
With pencils sharpened, notebook ready:
"Baker, Baker, this is Able . . ."
Then words come tumbling in a flood
Or one by one like drops of blood,

Or sometimes none at all, depending.
In finding what there is to say,
In sitting, quietly attending,
Until *they're* there, between blue lines:
Then letting them go on their way
Or fitting them to my designs
In the sweet exercise of will,
Unbroken hours pass, until

Through thin walls I hear my neighbors
On either side decide, "We're done!"
And me? I've little for my labors.
Four lines that seem less than terrific:
"Outside as a declining sun
Takes aim at [*aims at?*] the Pacific,
A posted notice quickly fills
With names of those who'll walk the hills . . .

And as I join those who assemble
In the clearing, blue jays chide
The visitors that gawk and shamble,
Unlike the Californians, who
Take walks like this one in their stride
And are, by now, accustomed to
Nasturtium leaves like manhole covers
And mates who *like* their spouses' lovers;

Those of us here for the first time
Find it all marvelously strange
And overdose on the sublime,
As even now my mind's eye traces
A sinuously curving range
Covered with dun-colored grasses
Below an ocean glimpsed in slivers,
Whose first appearance gave me shivers.

And then got me to worrying
That all such marvels have their price:
Would work lose out to sightseeing
And vinous, late-night conversations

In this terrestrial paradise,
This ranch that raises expectations,
And where the only thing amiss
Is my concern that nothing is?

Am I engaging in this blather
Merely to hide my awkwardness
As unfamiliar spirits gather?
Sojourners in-and-out-of state
Know that a question will suffice
To prompt the inarticulate,
And strangers to each others' aims
Find common ground in dropping names:

No one at first knows anyone,
But this one *once* knew that one's *ex,* and
A moment later we've begun
The questioning that soon reveals
Ramifications which extend
Beyond the moment and much else,
To distant galaxies which glow
With reruns of *The Lucy Show* . . .

I'll get to know some neighbors better,
And after going on my way
I'll keep in touch by phone or letter
With first a few, then two, then one,
Until a letter sent one day
Returns to me, address unknown.
Or was it not sent anyhow?
But that's enough of them for now:

As we set out on our walk,
I fumble the new terms, intent
On unfamiliar leaf and stalk
Expressed in Latin or in Greek
Words lifted out of what they meant
To join the English we now speak;
Fresh labels lovingly applied
By Herb, our knowledgeable guide

To unfamiliar plants and trees:
Here's Artemisia, there's French Broom,
That's Hemlock, sipped by Socrates;
And this bright orange-petaled mound
Is Monkeyweed, in frantic bloom;
And on the hillsides that surround,
There's growth too tall for underbrush:
Baccharis, called Coyotebush.

I quickly scribble down the names
And usually a remark
Disposing of disputed claims,
As one by one, Herb settles each
Aboard the taxonomic ark
And tucks it in—then tells us which
Of them prefer to creep and crawl,
Which imitate suburban sprawl;

Which cling to roadsides, which invade
The meadows and choke out old growth;
Which do best in partial shade
And which are partial to the sun,

And which impartially like both;
And in his meditation on
The brief lives of the flowers
He finds a paradigm for ours,

A world like our own, comprised
Of angrily competing nations,
Of colonists and colonized.
Through vegetable eons of
Warfare, conquests, exterminations,
Too green to cry, *We've had enough*
Of all this mindless grief!
Now wait: It's easy to exaggerate.

But what is this ungainly thing
Ahead of us? Thick limbs arrayed
In rags of bark inspiring
Legends deep-rooted in despair,
Stories of some great loser, flayed
Beyond redemption or repair,
Some Marsyas, securely bound
In great Lianas: run to ground,

He found himself (so many do)
Settling down into a place
He'd only thought of passing through:
A pulse of air stirred hollow bone,
And he by metamorphosis
Became this tree, called a *Madrone*;
The name, as usual, supplied
Us in passing by our guide.

What made me think of Marsyas,
Whose nerves a jealous god stripped bare?
Perhaps the heat that vaporizes
Oils of laurel, sage, and dill
And leaves them hanging in the air,
Their tangled scents a clue, until,
Though it's somewhere I've never been,
I feel I'm back in Greece again.

But would Greek poets in a chorus
Transported here cry, "Hold the flutes—
Eureka, fellows—that's Baccharis!"
Would Aristotle find the same
Essences and attributes
Present under either name?
Would hemlock growing in these hills
Have given Socrates the chills?

Is it appropriate to call
By foreign names the native rose?
And if we must give names at all,
Should haughty Dame Nomenclature
Eurocentrically impose
On the New World's unspoiled nature?
No: let our names all plainly come
From the American idiom,

Speech unhoused and unhousebroken,
Speech unadorned by ornament
And understood (if not yet spoken)
By cats and dogs—even by

Poets of xenophobic bent
Who'd cast a grim, suspecting eye
On anyone who would embarrass
A native with the name *Baccharis*.

Coyotebush sounds more demotic,
Though the first part is Nahuatl,
Which (to my ear) is as exotic
As is *Baccharis*—a metaphor
Not just unknown to Aristotle
But unconceived of heretofore,
Unless in the un-Aristote-
lian vision of Coyote,

A trickster who has many names,
And lends *his* to anonymous
Coyotes at coyote games;
No more than two of them could fit
Underneath each eponymous
Shrub to hide from one who's "it,"
Huddled together jowl by cheek
In feral bouts of hide-and-seek . . .

But I—or rather, this—digresses,
This poem, is it, in a style
That like a summer's breeze caresses,
Touches upon, the group that passes
Over a ridge in single file,
Parting a waist-high sea of grasses
Before the sun, declining west,
And shadows, lengthening, suggest

Another theme, so often used
That I was anxious to avoid it,
Afraid that I would be accused
Of terminal belatedness;
Ecclesiastes once employed it,
Borrowed, no doubt, from *Gilgamesh:*
Nothing is new under the sun,
And all is vanity we've done.

Thoughts such as these often occur
As shadows pull us to the brink
Of night, and vision starts to blur;
What's left for anyone to do,
And can I freshen up that drink?
Of course you can, I wish I knew—
But is it possible that we,
Who think ourselves *le dernier cri,*

And who collectively inherit
The forms all former ages shaped,
Can do no better than to parrot—
Or, as we say, "appropriate"—
Grand themes in styles once apt, now aped,
Once suitable, now second-rate?
And, as I asked before, must we,
Who think ourselves *le dernier cri,*

As we might say, "the latest thing,"
Inhabit a formal emptiness,
Grimly diminuendo-ing
Until the end, boys—or should we

Rent us a hall and self-express,
No matter how insensibly;
"Choose now, there are no other choices."
(This from a press of urgent voices.)

Isn't it possible to choose
Neither of those? Can't we restore
The Age of Innocence? Refuse
To abide by the archaic ban
Instituted long before
The Age of Irony began?
In short, return to that forbidden
Day-Care Center known as Eden,

Where our first parents make their way
On paths that wind through cunning mazes
In which their clueless footsteps stray;
Now pausing to consult the *Guide*
To Hosannas, Hymns, and Praises
(A book the Gideons provide);
Or wondering, beneath a tree,
What to put on for company.

But they're so easily delighted,
Who have no prospects that displease—
Imagine them at some unsighted
Locus classicus of love,
A mossy bank, a screen of trees
Resembling this alder grove
Where two unmet before will meet
While seeking refuge from the heat.

Imagine their new satisfaction!
Transparent, with no character
To propel them into action,
Uncompromised by pre-worn diction,
They simply *can't* be insincere:
Lacking most elements of fiction,
They fall back naturally on setting
As they get on with the begetting.

Such getting on begets the myth
Of prelapsarian innocence
We're all of us familiar with,
And, when we fall in love, believe:
That two may put off all pretense
And every purpose to deceive,
And find, when having come together,
Themselves possessed in one another.

Yet even here in paradise
Are intimations of times past,
Which our timeless myth denies:
Averted glances, words unspoken
Suggest that concord will not last,
The knot of tangled limbs be broken,
And new delight turn to dismay
With one another: while this may

Be paradise, it isn't Eden.
Or is it just that they're too late?
Whether upstanding or downtrodden,
Even the grass has a history

Whose character determines fate,
Which it must bow to, as must we.
But what of [INSERT NAME HERE]? You,
The fiction this is written to—

To whose low tastes I've often pandered,
Made insecure by your impatience—
By now, I'm sure of it, you've wandered
Off to find greater thrills and spills
Than these abstruse ruminations,
These sugar-coated quinine pills
Of mine are able to provide—
Ah, but you're here still at my side!

You haven't gone at all—and even
If you *had* left me for a moment,
That's easily and soon forgiven.
But joy in your return is blended
With the renewal of this torment,
For without you I might have ended
This poem here and now, set free
From my incessant anxiety:

Ambivalent are our dealings:
I summon up and soon discard
Resentment, gratitude, hurt feelings.
Nevertheless, without you, I
Might wind up in the *avante-garde*,
Generic Reader—which is why
The chief complaint I have of you
Is that so far you're far too few.

But now we should be going in:
While we've enjoyed our stop-time solo,
Others, invisible, have been
At work: I hear a swelling chorus
In the ranch house kitchen far below;
Dinner will be waiting for us,
But if we hurry down, I think
There may be time to have a drink,

Before we gather all around
The table, headed up by Beryl,
Our English cook, who's very fond
Of serving us exotic roasts
Of flesh predominantly feral,
From local game farms or (she boasts)
The road itself: a joke, we say,
But look for skid marks anyway.

And finding none, blunt hunger's edge
On what the kitchen has provided
(Possum in plum sauce with 3 veg);
Now conversations may resume,
New intimacies are confided
And circulate around the room,
Until the vocal current weakens,
And slumber, or some number, beckons.

Soon those who've paired off disappear:
Where do they go? They go to town,
While the unpartnered linger here.
There comes a moment when, returning

To my own room, I lay me down
With the few lines I wrote this morning,
Racked by bouts of indecision
And second thoughts about revision,

And most of all—the hour's late—
How will I bring *this* to an end?
It threatens not to terminate,
Although its day is all but over:
We've seen the sun's flat disc descend
Beyond the hills, go undercover
Preparing for its next assignment.
And so, if my announced design meant

Anything, it should have meant
Closure, conclusion, *Buona sera!*
Perhaps it has its own intent,
This poem does, and now rehearses
Developments I'm unaware of,
For parthenogenetic verses
To strut to, uninhibited,
While I lie sleeping in my bed,

And the few problems that still linger
(Such as the one of finding closure)
Are solved (though I don't lift a finger),
As walls and ceiling liquify
(A *stanza* slipping out of measure?)
To show the stars against the sky
Indifferent to limb and breath
As to the nothing underneath

The nothingness that seems to be
An endless, unmodulated roar
Our voices must accompany—
But this is getting serious!
Doctor, I've had this dream before:
Moonlight, winter, a delirious
Traveler teetering on the edge
Of a crumbling sandstone ledge

Dreams, it may be, of a way back
And goes back that way in his dream
Until he dreams himself awake
Among appearances deceiving:
Two of him there, as it would seem,
And then one evanesces, leaving
The other with—with what profound
Wisdom drawn up from underground?

What is he struggling to say?
Awake, I've lost it, but I'll find
My poem on a silver tray
Beside the bed: the ink still wet,
The paper warm, the work unsigned;
Before I put my name to it,
Let me compose, in other words,
The residence that it affords:

Four walls, a ceiling and a floor,
A desk, a bed, a chair or two;
One wall of glass, a sliding door
That leads onto a balcony

From which I have a lightening view
Of the low hills in front of me
And now an ending as the sun
Rising shows a new day begun.

III. Then, as It Happened

We say time passes, but we pass
And time remains. We are the motion
Of wind through levelheaded grass,
Fire that quickens the slow hill,
A cloud's shadow on the ocean;
Always we are what is unstill:
For all the length of our days
We are what passes, not what stays.

Then as it happened, I flew back
Into my interrupted life,
With Beryl's box lunch in my pack:
Half of a nicely roasted hare
(Still warm when lifted off the drive)
Ripe olives, riper cheese, a pear;
A pleasing bottle of Merlot,
And planks of fragrant sourdough.

Now I'm the envy of my flightmates,
Who stare, disconsolate, or prod
The mess of nutrients and nitrates
There on the tray before them, slowly
Congealing in a plastic pod
That swarms with virulent *E. coli* . . .
On either side, I realize,
A traveler with hungry eyes

Compels me to consume in stealth
Beryl's impressive provender,
Or open up and share the wealth:
I'm seldom one to split a hare,
And it's not easy to surrender
The last fruits of my being-there,
But how can I not? Three of us dine
Sumptuously and then recline

Before we presently withdraw
From company: *Aisle* finds his place in
Grisham's new proof of Gresham's Law,
While an expanded *Window Seat*
Dozing, mumbles, "Fortnum . . . Mason . . ."
Alone at thirty thousand feet,
A conscious dust mote in the hand
Of powers I cannot command,

I find myself revisiting
Conversations long since ended,
Revising them and editing
The balls I'd fumbled on occasion
Out of the sound-mix I'd intended;
Each irrefutable new version
Severed from its ahem, ahems,
Glitters with aphoristic gems.

Such harmless fixes and inventions
Are how we turn the tables on
Life that nixes our intentions;

The arguments we've deconstrued
When all at last is said and done,
Spring up again, revived, renewed
In thrust and parry and riposte-
Now interrupted by our host:

"The moth that figures in your myth
About the end?" (Referring to
The moth I ended Part I with)
"It's altogether clear that this
Moth represents the poet, who
Is changed, just like a chrysalis—
The open book he rises from
Must mean our moth is a bookworm—

"Or else the book is his cocoon—
That reading suits the image better,
For in my view, the poet's one
Who brings order to the world's waste
Bit by bit, letter by letter,
And each laboriously traced
On his own flesh, until he's dressed in
An artful weave of self-expression.

"One final transformation must
See him released forevermore
From the last trace of mortal dust:
The ties that bind him to his text
Must be completely slipped, before—"
(Rilke will be decanted next,
I hear it coming) "—he roams free
In realms of pure transcendency."

Interpretation is an act
Of generosity, and I
Can hardly but be grateful. Tact
And gratitude at once combine
In what I hope will satisfy:
"That figure now is yours, not mine."
A wiggle gets me off the hook.
Another's reading sees the book

As one that poets often get
Thrown at them by critics who
Rise up, determined not to let
Our follies unreproven go:
"Do just as *Theory* tells you to,
Obey when *History* says *no*—
And since *we're* all that matters, why
Must you keep writing poetry?

"Why don't you give up? Go away!
You aren't needed anymore:
The artist is a stowaway,
Feeding upon the silken cloth
And arcane notions we import,
A houligan, a parasite—a moth!
When we eliminate this pest,
Our Emperor will be well-dressed . . ."

You're raising *that* again, I see:
Is it unfair of me to note
A certain, well, transparency
In your designs? Yet no one tries

Harder than I do: I blink and squint,
At times I've even closed both eyes—
In short, I do my level best
To see the Emperor as dressed.

But something in me keeps me from
The thought that seeing is obeying.
It may be that I'm just too dumb.
It may be nothing other than
That I am most myself when playing
The obdurate contrarian
Who *will* say no, whose days are spent
Refusing to give blind assent.

Not one among us without doubt
Would be at all inclined to choose
A gift one would do well without,
Unless one *wanted* to be labeled
Obscure, archaic, and obtuse
By the much-differently-abled;
And yet this disability
Of saying what one cannot see

Might have a useful application
Elsewhere, in another setting:
A space arises from negation
(A cell? A suite? Descriptions vary:
"That fireplace!" "The central heating!"
"Exotic!" "Rather ordinary . . .)
Resistant shape, wherein one may
Imagine what one has to say,

And though the many will ignore it,
As by appointment or by chance
Someone will appear before it
(For someone always has, so far)
Who'll find this measured utterance
Appealing, and (the door ajar)
Will wander in, alone, unheeding,
As to—oh, a poetry reading,

Whose audience consists of . . . you.
There's only one of you, I see.
One would have hoped there might be two.
One ought to be outnumbered by
One's audience, don't you agree?
The two of us, then? You and I?
Will no one else be dropping in?
I thought as much. Then let's begin . . .

While one by one my readers find
A room to stay in for a while,
A place within the work of mind,
I dream about a group that passes
Over a ridge in single file
Until our steward comes demanding
That I prepare for our landing;

And in the moments that remain
Of this transcontinental flight,
I bless the powers that sustain
Us as our fragile ark descends
Toward lives we will resume tonight,
And bless the darkness that extends
Beyond us and proposes what
We will all come to, no doubt but.

IV.
from STEAL THE BACON

COMPLAINT OF THE NIGHT WATCHMAN

The tower they are building turns to speech,
Narrows almost to nowhere, nearing completion.
The builders have no grasp of their tower's reach
And more fall silent as each new addition
Leaves them all left with less and less to stand on,
Becoming fictions with each winding story.
It wasn't this that the builders had planned on
When they imagined for themselves the glory
Of this unparalleled erection, a tower
That would rise to heaven, making man divine.
But they ignored or perhaps had forgotten the power
That merely human speech has to undermine
Godlike achievement. Grave misapprehension:
Now word of Babel—that is their name for it—
Flies on the four winds, and every vagrant mention
Brings news of their inflated claim for it
To heaven, where this pleases not at all.
The gods confer about this grand delusion.
They do so even now. It must soon fall,
And those who'd build it fall into confusion
Of language, and the race of builders scatter.
With them will go odd pieces of the rubble
To stand for failed unity. And of more matter,
Tongues that will turn their failure into fable.

STEAL THE BACON

"First Flossie . . . then Sean . . . and now Moe . . ." Surely their brightest
Are bright enough to have already noticed
That every morning the one who last molded elastic
Bones and went pouring like mercury under
The molding does not return. Surely someone must wonder,
"What in God's name ever becomes of them?"
Trap crushes snout and hind legs tap out a spastic
Coda, diminuendo, on cold linoleum,

Far from the muzzy warmth of the nest, that supportive nexus
Of sensual mouse life. Those are x's
That were his eyes, or hers. And doesn't anyone notice
A cherished aunt or uncle's sudden
Vanishing act? "Let's see now . . . Flossie disappeared one
Night last week . . . was she the first? Was Sean?
Mousebrain! Why can't I keep them in order? I only know this:
That one by one we seem to be drawn

Forward against our wills, tho' scampering brightly
Toward that narrow strip of light we
All of us fear. Beyond it, the high kitchen table;
Delectable odors that overcome Reason
And Prudence; blistery fragments of grilled cheese on
Stale crust; and the fatty bacon
That somehow kills, in the legend which is, whether fact or fable,
The nightmare from which we would awaken.

Real mice in silence rise to the subtly baited
Trap not caring whether free or fated.
Springy gray squealers pulse with indecision,
Wrinkling their vulnerable noses
As they try to answer the question this poised engine poses.
And then either scamper back under the wall
Or stay to play steal the bacon—a game in which steely precision
Cracks down on mouseflesh or down on nothing at all.

AFTER THE RAPE OF THE SABINE WOMEN

They never speak of what happened during their capture,
The house-to-house searches, the violent seizures,
The brisk allotment of women to sausage-faced soldiers
Ripping off bronze-plated armor in innocent rapture:
But of some last choice made earlier that morning,
The lover or book chosen for wit, for beauty,
Or for idleness torn out of hand without warning
And flung away broken.
                    Now, in the streets of the city,
They move with an air of abstraction, pushing their infants
Before them, like so many dowsers searching for water;
Breasts drip with milk, knuckles whiten on a stroller's
Chromium bar: a single moment's confusion
Leaves one a hostage forever, inscribing invisible,
Momentary lines in the language of desire.

DESIGN

Lines scored across this fragment of a bone
Worked by a smaller piece of sharpened stone

Gripped firmly in a hand now dust may tell
How to apportion time or cast a spell;

But whether they were calendar or curse,
The scratched recording of some deathless verse

Or none of the above, we cannot say:
Can only say the readings that we take

Of this now enigmatic instrument
Indicate aim, purpose, some meaning meant—

Meaning, in this case, goes against the grain,
Would not be noticed otherwise. Design,

Whether we find it legible or not,
Reveals itself in what is taken out,

A kind of absence in a thing designed
By which we recognize presence of mind.

A BURIAL AT SHANIDAR

Men of our kind, digging in the cellar
Of a cave, uncovered what was hidden:
Bones that from steeping in the earth's strong tea
For countless years had taken on its color.
But were those bones just tossed onto the midden,
Or had they been buried? A mystery.
The soiled fragments of a salvaged skull
At first said nothing but Neanderthal.

Bones in better repair, appearing beneath
That skull's dyed egg, allowed them to recover
A specimen long crippled by disease,
Worn out at forty, arthritic since his birth,
A burden on the group, which had, however,
Provided him with his necessities,
And afterward had buried him and mourned,
With ceremony—as our cavemen learned.

For when they sent the matter of that site
To be examined by a botanist
In Europe, she immediately found
The remnants of a grave—a shallow pit
Lined with pine branches, on which he'd been placed,
Before the group had scattered all around
What never could have gotten there by chance:
Cornflowers, hollyhock, grape-hyacinth.

Their custom noted in the dried-out pollen
Of long gone flowers, dropped by hands the same,
As fleeting as the shadows on the wall
That flickered in firelight around the fallen;
How hesitantly, awkwardly they came
Forward to celebrate his funeral,
Those dim, unsightly ancestors of ours,
Clutching their little sprays of wildflowers

And uttering their almost human cries
Of unsuccess, as shambling, grotesque,
They stood around the figure in the grave
And mumbled what might have meant, *Take these,*
Which we have gathered at no little risk
In the wild places far beyond the cave.
We thought to honor you. The reasons why
Would perish with the last of them to die.

DOMESTIC INTERIOR

When I try to imagine the Garden
Of Eden, I see an upended cave,
Like the one which my son has created
Out of the now lidless cardboard carton
In which a neighbor's Frigidaire arrived,
And a woollen blanket, liberated
From an upstairs closet. Done with the chore
Of rearranging mental furniture,

He clambers into place and hunkers down
With the odors, those imaginary
Friends from an unimaginable past;
Warmed by his warmth, they come forth, voices drawn
Out of the blanket's faded memory,
Out of the threadbare fabric of that nest.

SPEECH AGAINST STONE

I watch the man in the schoolyard
As he brushes a flat coat of institutional beige
Over a wall brilliant with childish graffiti,
      Turning a fresh page,

A surface the kids will respray
As soon as his back is turned. I suppose I should
Be thinking—as any upstanding, taxpay-
      ing citizen would—

Of the money and man-hours spent
Covering up these phosphorescent hues
And adolescent cries of discontent;
      But as he continues,

I find myself divided:
The huge roller goes sweeping on over the stone,
And I see in what he is doing a labor
      Not unlike my own

When I erase, letter by letter,
The words I've just written, in the hope that all
My scratching out may summon something better—
      And besides, the wall

Surely approves of this work,
For who can believe that it would choose to say
FUCK THE WORLD or FAT ANTHONY'S A JERK
      Or DMF JOSE?

No, left to its own devices,
The wall would stand forever an unlettered book,
Prepared to meet eternity's inspection
        With its own blank look.

But that, of course, is what summons
The hidden children out of their hiding places—
That inviting blankness as the janitor finally covers
        Up the last traces,

Gathers together his painting
Gear and goes clattering off. No sooner gone
Than they return to renew the ancient complaint
        Of speech against stone,

Spelling out—misspelling, often—
The legends of the heart's lust for joy and violence
In waves that break upon but will not soften
        The cliffs of obdurate silence.

A HAPPY ENDING FOR THE LOST CHILDREN

One of their picture books would no doubt show
The two lost children wandering in a maze
Of anthropomorphic tree limbs: the familiar crow

Swoops down upon the trail they leave of corn,
Tolerant of the error of their ways.
Hand in hand they stumble onto the story,

Brighteyed with beginnings of fever, scared
Half to death, yet never for a moment
Doubting the outcome that had been prepared

Long in advance: Girl saves brother from oven,
Appalling witch dies in appropriate torment;
Her hoarded treasure buys them their parents' love.

*   *   *

"As happy an ending as any fable
Can provide," squawks the crow, who had expected more:
Delicate morsels from the witch's table.

It's an old story—in the modern version
The random children fall to random terror.
You see it nightly on the television:

Cameras focus on the lopeared bear
Beside the plastic ukulele, shattered
In a fit of rage—the lost children are

Found in the first place we now think to look:
Under the fallen leaves, under the scattered
Pages of a lost children's picture book.

*   *   *

But if we leave terror waiting in the rain
For the wrong bus, or if we have terror find,
At the very last moment the right train,

Only to get off at the wrong station—
If we for once imagine a happy ending,
Which is, as always, a continuation,

It's because the happy ending's a necessity,
It isn't just a sentimental ploy—
Without the happy ending there would be

No one to tell the story to but the witch,
And the story is clearly meant for the girl and boy
Just now about to step into her kitchen.

E. S. L.

My frowning students carve
Me monsters out of prose:
This one—a gargoyle—thumbs its contemptuous nose
At how, in English, subject must agree
With verb—for any such agreement shows
   Too great a willingness to serve,
      A docility

Which wiry Miss Choi
Finds un-American.
She steals a hard look at me. I wink. Her grin
Is my reward. *In his will, our peace, our Pass:*
Gargoyle erased, subject and verb now in
   Agreement, reach object, enjoy
      Temporary truce.

Tonight my students must
Agree or disagree:
America is still a land of opportunity.
The answer is always, uniformly, *Yes*—even though
"It has no doubt that here were to much free,"
   As Miss Torrico will insist.
      She and I both know

That Language binds us fast,
And those of us without
Are bound and gagged by those within. Each fledgling polyglot
Must shake old habits: tapping her sneakered feet,
Miss Choi exorcises incensed ancestors, flout-
   ing the ghosts of her Chinese past.
      Writhing in the seat

Next to Miss Choi, Mister
Fedakis in anguish
Labors to express himself in a tongue which
Proves *Linear B* to me, when I attempt to read it
Later. They're here for English as a Second Language,
    Which I'm teaching this semester.
        God knows they need it,

And so, thank God, do they.
    The night's made easier
By our agreement: I am here to help deliver
Them into the good life they write me papers about.
English is prerequisite for that endeavor,
    Explored in their nightly essays
        Boldly setting out

To reconnoiter the fair
    New World they would enter:
Suburban Paradise, the endless shopping center
Where one may browse for hours before one chooses
Some new necessity—gold-flecked magenta
    Wallpaper to re-do the spare
        Bath no one uses,

Or a machine which can,
    In seven seconds, crush
A newborn calf into such seamless mush
As a *mousse* might be made of—or our true sublime:
The gleaming counters where frosted cosmeticians brush
    Decades from the allotted span,
        Abrogating time

As the spring tide brushes
A single sinister
Footprint from the otherwise unwrinkled shore
Of America the Blank. In absolute confusion
Poor Mister Fedakis rumbles with despair
And puts the finishing smutches
To his conclusion

While Miss Choi erases:
One more gargoyle routed.
Their pure, erroneous lines yield an illuminated
Map of the new found land. We will never arrive there,
Since it exists only in what we say about it,
As all the rest of my class is
Bound to discover.

EASTER SUNDAY, 1985

> *To take steps toward the reappearance alive of the*
> *disappeared is a subversive act, and measures will be*
> *adopted to deal with it.*
> —General Oscar Mejia Victores,
>   President of Guatemala

In the Palace of the President this morning,
The General is gripped by the suspicion
That those who were disappeared will be returning
In a subversive act of resurrection.

Why do you worry? The disappeared can never
Be brought back from wherever they were taken;
The age of miracles is gone forever;
These are not sleeping, nor will they awaken.

And if some tell you Christ once reappeared
Alive, one Easter morning, that he was seen—
Give them the lie, for who today can find him?

He is perhaps with those who were disappeared,
Broken and killed, flung into some ravine
With his arms safely wired up behind him.

JULY 1914

after Anna Akhmatova

I

A stench of burning. For the past four weeks
The peat in the marshes has been smoldering.
The timid aspen bough no longer quakes
At the slightest breeze, the birds no longer sing.

God has abandoned us. We've had no rain
Since Eastertime: the blackened wheat is dead.
A crippled man came into the courtyard once
To prophesy, and this is what he said:

"Horrors approach us—soon the earth will swell
With those who have died of plague and famine;
Earthquakes will open up new paths to hell,
And in the sky strange portents will be seen.

But the brutal invaders cannot destroy
This land entirely—no, they will fail:
God's holy mother will conceal their joy
And our sorrow with a pure white veil . . .

II

From burning woods, the smell of juniper.
All throughout the village, despairing wives
And widows weep for the fallen soldiers,
Weep for the children, weep for their own lives.

At last the unrelenting Father yields,
And the crops are drenched. Not at all in vain,
Those prayers of ours: the blackened fields
Run with our blood. We had asked for rain.

Such emptiness. The barren sky descends,
And in the dark one hears a frightened voice:
"O they have numbered Thy most holy wounds,
And for Thy garments they are casting dice . . .

III
After the buying, selling, looting, and betrayal,
The batlike wing of death led us to where
Anguished jaws were shivering a fleshless skull .
Yet what we feel is nothing like despair:

Out of the dark woods close by the town, our days
Are suffused with the scent of wild cherry,
And at night the flickering stars parade
In regiments across the summer sky.

Unutterable holiness bows down
Over the ruins. It was always near,
But we didn't know this, we had never known,
Though we longed from earliest times for it to appear.

"GRACE, SECRETS, MYSTERIES . . ."
Fatima, 1917

Three scowling, hamfisted faces
Squint at the alien camera suspiciously:
Lucia, Jacinta, and Francisco,
   Monsters of piety

And self-abasement, fresh
Green shoots grafted to the ancient stem
Of penitence. They mortify their serious flesh
   Until Our Lady must caution them:

"Drink stale ditchwater, share
Your lunches with poorer children or your sheep;
Enough, no more—my Son is troubled when you wear
   Thick ropes to cut you in your sleep . . .

But what is enough, when nothing
Seems to be? When no amount of suffering suffices
To close the gates of hell?
                                Lucia hangs
   Above the agonizing faces

Of the damned, a scum of souls
Weightlessly drifting on a sea of fire.
What is enough? Demons rake the coals
   And waves of flame leap higher.

But who will heed the warning
Of these devout, uneducated children?
Only those who are themselves already burning
   In the earth's slow cauldron,

Gnarled as the olives and scrub oaks
That have learned to live almost without water
In the meager hills where every pile of rocks
    Commemorates its virgin martyr—

Attacked, of course, by the atheist
Mayor, whose strident printing press bids faction
Unite with faction: "REPUBLICANS! Awaken and resist
    The seductive music of reaction!"

The Great War widens and Portugal
Begins to slide: conscripts herded first to Mass,
Then to the trenches. Lucia's twin cousins inhale
    Barbed hooks of mustard gas,

Return to proclaim that the scattered
Innocents of every explosion
Limb by luckless limb will be regathered
    On the Day of Resurrection;

And at Lourdes, Anatole France,
"Quaffing the cynic's cup to the last, bitter dregs,"
Faced with a long wallful of jettisoned crutches and canes,
    Asked, "What—are there no wooden legs?"

MANDELSTAM IN TRANSIT

My age, my beast, is there one who
Will lift his head to meet your stare,
Or with his living blood repair
That fractured spine of yours for you?
Long years of suffering. Now this:
A spineless, parasitic crew
Herding us on toward the abyss.

Until he's finished in his grave,
As long as he has breath, a man
Must feel, above his covered spine,
A gentle rippling, like a wave.
But now the tender cartilage
Of childhood is broken, the crown
Of first life crushed in pointless rage.

For life at last to break away,
For the new world to take root,
The hollow music of the flute
Must link up each disjointed day.
But the age is troubled by its dreams:
A serpent winding underfoot
Hisses the true music of the times.

Green shoots, my age, will once again
Rise up, new buds will once more swell,
My pitied dear, my beautiful,
Despite your agonizing pain—
What lies in your deceitful smile!
You turn back, staring at the stain
Of blood on snow, mile after mile.

TO THE LIVING BAIT

The hook is now firmly embedded between your shoulder-
     blades: that was the sharp pain you may have felt
          just a moment ago.
Your hands and feet will feel a little bit colder,
     But there should be no pain at all now. Please signal
          if there is pain. No?

Good. Then let us continue. At our first session
     Together, you brought up those questions we've come
          to expect:
"Why am I here? Why should I have been chosen?"
     By now you will have had more than sufficient time to
          reflect

On our responses, which ranged from the artfully shaded
     Moderately evasive equivocation to the openfaced,
          outright lie.
"There was no reason at all," you will have concluded,
     "It was an accident that brought me here." Please signal
          if you disagree.

No, nothing required that you should have been lifted
     Out of the flow and not someone else. For if we had
          needed to use
Someone clever or goodlooking or in any way gifted,
     We would have left you at home in bed, watching the
          evening news,

Since you weren't any of those things ever,
     Were you? And if you had been, that too would be
          perfectly fine,

Though you would be thinking, "Because I am clever
    Or gifted or handsome, I find myself here at the end
        of the line."

Not so. For nothing more is ever required
    Of those, like yourself, who advance to the final
        selection
Than a perfectly normal need to be desired
    And an equally normal, even commendable,
        fear of rejection.

These suit you, briefly, to our purpose. Which is
    Merely to learn if anything under the surface might
        be so provoked
To anger or hunger by your insensible twitches
    That it will answer your need with its own, and find
        itself hooked.

Are you ready now? Please don't bother replying.
    Thanks to you, so far everything has gone just
        as we planned.
This will not comfort you while you are dying.
    Don't think we don't understand.

LANDSCAPE WITHOUT HISTORY

I. Early Morning at Hartwell Pond, Vermont

Finding in the trap beneath the table
An ounce or so of fur, with one eye closed
And one incongruously made of blood,
I set out juice and milk and cereal,
But not, of course, before I have disposed
Of the mouse from whom the mountains of our food
Were kept by just this tiny piece of bacon;
A morsel that snapped back as it was taken
Cruelly pinned that ruby to its eye
And crushed its snout and snuffed its whisker tips.
After I wash my hands clean of the beast,
I turn to the stove: now eggs begin to fry
In the sweet butter and now coffee drips.
I call my children down to share this feast.

II. At the Museum in St. Johnsbury

In the museum at St. Johnsbury,
This hollow stump, a rodent Quonset hut,
Was artfully turned into a freeze-dried
Diorama: mice without motion scurry
About in a similitude of what-
ever they had been up to when they died;
As part of this incongruous arrangement,
They demonstrate death's permanent estrangement,
Caught in a moment without wit to spare
A single one

Ancient figures of Pompeii
Immobilized two thousand years ago

Their cries left hanging in the smoky air

All but their last gestures burned away
Under that warm and suffocating snow

III. Composition with Rocks and Grasses

Heedless, a glacier chiseled this arrangement
Of three pieces of shale as an afterthought
To the work of gouging out the pond itself;
With all but energy for small change spent,
The ice slid back until these steps were cut
Out of the pond's steeply descending shelf
And tilted up. Another arrangement made
With local grasses provided stem and blade,
Yielding diagonals that comb the three
Slabs of grey bedrock with strands of gold and green
To soften the severity of the composition
And introduce a new complexity
As time follows through the spaces in between
The quickened rocks that now reflect each season.

IV. Late Afternoon at Hartwell Pond

When I first hear, then sight, the swiftly paced
Armed fighter streaking overhead, I wonder
Absently whether it's just another dress
Rehearsal, or the thing itself, at last.
As usual, for practice, I surrender
Myself and the ones I love as hostages
To the whining echoes of its aftermath.
I have rehearsed surrender in the path
Of our once-flung, inexorable weapons
Often enough, while a finger paused between
Go back to base, go on to megakill—
Blips on a screen. Our helplessness sharpens
The shark's tooth against us, as against the green
Wall at the pond's back, now quivering, now still.

MAKING FACES

for Peter Schumann

*We begin to see that it is better to keep life fluid and
changing than to try to hold it down fast in heavy
monuments. . . . Give us things that are alive and flexible,
which won't last too long and become an obstruction and a
weariness.* —D. H. Lawrence

I. THE WORLD

Every year there is a big parade
In Barton, Vermont, on the Fourth of July
When we celebrate the red white and blue—
During the course of which we see displayed
Some of the Pentagon's old weaponry;
An armored car, a Sherman tank or two
Add martial tone to the festive atmosphere:
Behind them come the Bread & Puppet Theatre,
Beginning with someone in a horse's head
Who's holding up a sign that says, THE WORLD,
As though the world were next in their procession,
Or their procession were the world instead.
And next to the horse there walks a little girl
Ringing a schoolbell for our attention:

The world we see approaching is a cart
Drawn by puppet oxen, their huge necks bent,
Their tranquil heads sweeping from side to side;
The world is filled with artless works of art,
Miniature figures that must represent
The people of the world out for a ride.
And the cart so full of them that one might say

No one at all has been left home today.
The world has drawn beside us now and soon
Will pass us by as the clouds pass us by
Overhead. The clouds move at their own pace
And so to us they hardly seem to move,
Those ghostly gray-white oxen of the sky
Drawing the world through realms of empty space.

This world addresses the fragility
Of the only other one we have to live in,
Where the marble-breasted laborers grow weak
And stumble to their knees and shortly die;
Where the poor must eat the stones that they are given
And the little painted figures fall and break;
And the extraordinary cloud-drawn cart
We thought would last forever comes apart.
What happens next in the parade, we ask?
We haven't long to wait before our answer:
Behind the cart drawn by the puppet oxen
Comes a stilted figure in a jackal mask,
Pounding on a drum! This dog-faced dancer
Raises a clangorous, dissonant tocsin—

II. THE END OF THE WORLD

We've practiced it too often in our age
To see it merely as the subtraction
Of bird from tree, of tree from earth, of earth from space,
As one erases letters from a page.
Yet we still think of it as an abstraction,
Something that isn't likely to take place—
Although it's taken place at places called
Guernica, Hiroshima, Buchenwald.
We think of the unthinkable with ease,

We've had such practice of it for so long;
And speak of it in ways which help conceal
From ourselves the dark realities
That numb the mind and paralyze the tongue.
And now in the parade there comes a skel-

etal figure on a skeletal horse,
Made of raw strips of pine lashed together.
Its attitude is distant yet familiar,
As though it were confident that in the course
Of time we'd get to know each other better.
It knows this in its bones, as we in ours.
(And so if Death should ever wave at you,
You may wave back, for you have manners too;
You needn't ask it to slow down or stop.)
It's followed by a Dragon, belching smoke;
One Demon drives it, another one attends
To the Great Devourer who sits on top,
Quietly enjoying some huge cosmic joke—
And that is the way The End of the World ends.

III. FIGHT THE END OF THE WORLD

Now Peter Schumann, dressed as Uncle Sam,
Strides down Main Street on his outrageous stilts
Carrying a sign that says, WATCH OUT!
A younger Uncle Sam prances around him,
Intricately weaving subtle steps
Under his teacher's exaggerated strut—
"They make it look so easy," someone says.
They dance before a ragtime band that plays
Molto con brio, more or less on key;
For there are many fine musicians in it
And they raise a joyful noise unto the Lord

Of all creation. The heart willingly
Gives its assent, but mind says, Wait a minute—
Is this how we're to Fight the End of the World?

—By making faces at appalling forces
And marching off to the Parade Grounds with
One's friends and neighbors, honest country folk
Changed into demons, dogs and demi-horses,
Or into oxen who present the world as myth,
Straining together underneath their yoke?
— By building things so that they cannot last
Unreasonably long? By honoring the past,
But raising up no wearisome immense
Rock for all ages? By rudely waking
The child-in-us and teaching it to play?
By going with the grain and not against?
By shaping our daily bread and baking
Thick-crusted loaves of it to give away?

We've seen The World as it was passing through,
And monstrous Death the world-devouring,
And a man on stilts, whose artistry astounded;
And now we have a sanitation crew
Sweeping and shoveling up dragon dung,
Leaving the street as spotless as they'd found it.
My questions beg an answer, as do I.
Some kind of answer may be given by
The Garbageman who shakes hands with my son
And daughter, then goes back to join his friends;
Or the Washerwoman in her faded dress,
On a holiday from work that's never done,
With whom, most fittingly, the pageant ends:
As she passes by, her sign says only, YES

V.
from PASSAGES FROM FRIDAY

PASSAGES FROM FRIDAY

In a little Time, I began to speak
to him, and teach him to speak to me;
having sav'd him on the 6th Day of the Week,
I made him know that his Name was to be

Friday; *I thought it right to call him so*
for the Memory of the Time; in the same Way
I taught him to say Master, *then let him know*
from this Day on, that was to be my Name.

I
With my owne thoro' un-Worthyness
all Ways befor my Face I turn to
this burthensom Task which nevertheless
being decided, *Viz.* That I must learn to

write as my *Master* did & so set down
tho' withowt any Hope of Recovery
from this inchanted Island to my owne
Nation whence taken in Captivity

som Yeers a go: That by the diligent
copying of Letters from his Bokes
now my owne I ha' further'd this Intent
to sutch Degree wher all most now it looks

if I may say so now it makes me think
that Heaven smiles upon my Enterprise:
That having got a Quantity of Ink
at no great Cost express'd from native Berries

sutch as may express my Native Wit
most suitably, if I may so conceive:
That having obtain'd sutch Fethers as are fit
to write with, once sharpen'd, I will now leave

all mis-givings as to my Ability
& here invoke all-mighty *Providence:*
That having from my *Master* a Supply
of What to write on, I will now commence

with an Accownt of my Deliverance
as this commenc'd my *new* or 2nd Life;
for, being ignorant of *Providence*
& its Design, I cling'd to the Belief

that thos seiz'd in War-fare cou'd be eaten;
this, I had learn'd, was what my *God* intended:
So, when my owne Nation was defeated
& I took Prisoner, it seem'd my Life was ended;

truss'd up & cast into a War-Canoo
I lay as one all ready Dead & thought
ownly of, *What my Enemy wou'd do.*
Soon at this Island I was abruptly brought

to Sacrifice, as one by 1 my 3
Fellowes were knock'd down, cut open & burn'd:
One still a live, twisting so in Agony
that it a mews'd my Captor, the Fellow turn'd

to watch the Sport: Up I leap & race
as swiftly as I can a long the Shoar:
A Cry goes up: Two of my Foes give Chace:
I run from them till I can run no more

when suddenly a Cross my Path ther flies
what seems a Mountain, cover'd all in Hair!
I tumble Grownd-ward, a trembling with Surprise:
Have I escap'd the Snell but for the Snare?

This *Mountain* proves *Volcano,* belching Fire
that strikes the foremost of my Persuers Dead
at which the 2nd one runs off in Terror;
I place the *Masters* Foot upon my Head.

II
My Beginning begun, I must begin agayn
for, tho' my *Master* is no longer a live,
his Spirit guides the Movement of my Pen
a Cross this Sheet, commanding me: *To give*

a true Account of owr Life together
in all Particulars: How each Day was spent
from 1st Light, when I go off to gather
Fewel for the Fire lay'd owt Side his Tent

then fetch his Cloathes for him & lay them owt:
Then leve him be now: Run off to prepare
his Goats-Flesh Stewe; this done, I hear him showt:
Bring him his Jugg: I fetch it in & pour

him a great Supp to drink, whilst he dresses
& then attend him till his Stewe is eaten
& then if all has not been as he pleases
as like as not poor *Friday* will get beaten;

then off to tend the Flock whos swolne Dams
bleating together urgently complain
of my Neglect; an Howre on my Hams
& thence to gather up what Scraps remain

after my *Master*; next to weed the Corn
which occupies my Time befor his Dinner
must be prepar'd; so passes the Morn;
It is because poor Friday *is a Sinner*

that he must spend his Days Gain-fully toiling,
my *Master* tells me; I slice his Bread & Chees
& bast with Grees the Joynt of Goat-Flesh broiling;
whil he has Dinner, *Friday* takes his Ease.

The after Noon was spent a frighting Game;
Parots especially he lov'd to kill,
for, having taught 1 once to say his Name,
that one, escaping, had pass'd on the Skill

to others of the brightly Fether'd Race;
so then, wherever in the Woods we go
from Tree to Tree a Head of us they chace
crying, *Robinson   Robinson   Crusoe*

Heedless of wasted Powder when he's vext
he fires off his Peeces 1 by 1
whil *Parots* fly from one Tree to the next
crying, *Crusoe   Crusoe   Robinson*

III

I mind 1 Time we bilded us a Raft
which, he say'd was, *A Work of no little Art*;
but the Islands Magick overcame his Craft
& the first Tide that took it, shook it a Part

& left the Peeces scatter'd on the Shoar;
for the Island held him firmly in its Grip
& wou'd not let go. It was not long befor
he had a nother Plan: *We wou'd bild a Ship*

owt of a hallow'd Log. Weeks must be spent
in searching of the Mountains for a Tree
that wou'd, in all Things, answer his Intent;
at last we found owr Selves a *Mahagonny*

which, he was sure, wou'd serve his Purpose well.
I guess'd it wou'd not, for when we found it
This Tree commenc'd groaning; when we began to fell
the lesser Trees that grew up all a round it

thes groan'd as well; I hear'd, but *Master* cou'd not;
earnestly I begg'd him, *To find a nother*
Tree, but he was adamant & wou'd not
hear of sutch Talk; a Cuffing for my Bother.

Now after we had cleer'd a Way the Grownd
came the felling of this prodigious Tree
no Tree at all, but a Womans Spryght imprison'd
which, as we cut it, moan'd so piteously

that owr Axes were enchanted by
the Sownd to sutch Degree that they lept back
in owr Hands, *as tho' they'd rather try*
owr Flesh than hers. After 1 sutch Attack

I saw that *Master* had been somewhat nick'd
by my owne Blade, which I at once let go;
I seiz'd his wounded Hand in mine & lick'd
the Blood a Way, as any Man wou'd do

owt of meer Affection; he wrenches loos
his Hand from mine & violently throes
me to the Grownd with scurrilous Abuse
& drives me from him with repeated Kicks & Blows.

IV
An Howre every Evening was given
to my Instruction, by which, however
imperfectly, I learn'd of *Hell & Heaven,*
the *Middle Way,* the *Pulley* & the *Lever*

& many a nother Use-full Invention,
astownding to me, who had mis-understood
so mutch befor; I soon form'd the Intention
of becoming as like my *Master* as I cou'd,

putting the *Cannibal* of earlier Yeers
behind me; and yet, my owne Ignorance
both hinder'd me & rais'd my *Masters* Fears
of my Savage Nature. *This* Callibans

a Canniball, he'd say: *No teaching him.*
Nevertheless, I learn'd how *God* and the *Devill*
must wage continuous War-Fare till the End of Time
or thenabowts, when *God* will putt an End to Evil;

& how to load & fire Fowling-Peeces
& cleen them after-ward; and how to cloathe
my self in Goat-Skins & to make Cheeses
from the Goats-Milk; and so on & so forth;

untill so mutch of what my *Master* knew,
I knew as well, quickly comprehending
even the meaner Things he taught me to do,
(Viz.) *cooking, cleaning-up, sewing & mending*;

and yet, tho' I did all I cou'd to plees,
learning to do & doing all I learn'd,
his Melancholy seem'd ownly to increes,
as tho' in his Innards a low Feaver burn'd.

V
When the Moons Light pours a Cross my Window-Sill
I spread my Writing owt upon my Knees
losing my Self for Howres in it till
my Wick of Oakum sputters in its Grees

& I nodd off. I had fell to dreaming
of once, when I, return'd to the Plantation
with Raizins for his Wine, I hear'd him screaming
as tho' persu'd by the whol *Caribb* Nation;

I rush'd froward, determin'd either to aid
him in his Struggle, or to fall besyde;
no one a peer'd to be at the Stockade
when I paws'd ther breefly for a Look inside;

rather I found him wher the Beasts were penn'd
& they all murther'd. He had slyt ther Throats
& as they twitch'd & skitter'd on the Grownd
he hack'd & slash'd at thes poor harm-less Goats

then order'd me to, *Bild a great big Fire*;
Naught may be sav'd of them at all, he say'd;
Let Flames consume ther Carckasses entire.
Now many of these Beasts were scarsly Dead

& others, all tho' dismember'd, still liv'd;
yet in my Fear, I none the less obey'd him,
sutch whippings & picklings as I receiv'd
whenever I objected or gainsay'd him.

Later, he say'd that the Goats had learn'd his Name
by listening to the escap'd *Parots*
& wou'd repeat it, braying, for a Game
till he was phrenzied. I say it was Spirits

that wait a bowt a Man to do him Harm
when they are able; thes infest the Island.
The Beasts being burn'd, he became quite calm
& for 3 Days remain'd a Loan in Silence.

When he came forth he went to the ruin'd Pen
& cast the Spirits owt in Peels of Laughter,
till at the last, he seem'd him-self agayn;
yet never wou'd he speak a bowt this after.

VI

But I digress here, having yet to tell
of, How we got the Tree down for owr *Canoo*;
after a whil, I offer'd to cast a Spell
to quieten the Womans Spirit, who

dwelt within it; I did a little Dance
& sprinkl'd the Grownd a round the Tree with Grain
mix'd with some Blood; the Spryght fell into Silence
& owr Axe-Blades obey'd us once agayn.

Master pretended not to see this at all
untill I had finish'd. We girdl'd it a round
then left it to bleed & dry; after severall
Weeks we came back & brought it to the Grownd.

Painfull Labour follow'd, for we must peel
all of the Bark a Way; then burn & scrape
the In-sides off with glowing Coals untill
it was hallow'd owt; then we must shape

the Out-side Part; and all of the Work we did,
owr endless toiling & incessant Care
serv'd only to show, *the Woman that was hid*;
at last her Figur was brought owt so cleer

that *Master* saw her, as he him-self confess'd;
and none of owr toiling cou'd efface
1 single Curve of Belly, Thigh, or Breast.
I judg'd her to be a Woman of my Race

by Virtue of her Colour, dark as the Grayn
of that *Mahagonee* in which we found her.
Perhaps she too was brought here to be slayn
& had escap'd when her Captors unbound her

for a Moment; and running off as I did,
but finding no *Master*, no Deliverance
from her persuing Enemies, she hid
her-self by taking leave of her Womans

Body & becoming at once a meer Tree;
her Roots sunk down, her Branches lifted high,
she blossom'd into a Security
that lasted untill we 2 hapn'd by.

VII
Of thos sever'd Branches I mutch later made
my *European Figur Fetisches*,
7 in Number, painted & array'd
a long the Shoar to ward off Savages

& to attrackt thos Shipps I some Times spy'd
at a great Distance; but they never came neer
all tho' at some Times the Savages did,
when, after War-fare they brought Captives heer

to feast upon them. I some Times discover'd
Remainders of ther Feasts upon the Sand
or in it, when my prodding Toe uncover'd
an eyeless Skull, a blackned Foot or Hand;

ther were 7 of thes Figurs, as I say'd;
and all of them stood facing owt to Sea
with Musket in one Hand & a naked Blade
in the other, scowling ferociously.

Often I try'd, but never succeeded,
in a wakening them; that Enterprise
was doom'd, for What my Europeans needed
was not my dancing, but a Shipps Supplies;

more Hats & Cloathes & shiny buckl'd Shoes,
more Axes, Muskets, Cannon & Gun-Powder,
more of sutch Goods than they cou'd ever use;
ownly sutch Abundance cou'd have rows'd them.

I danc'd abowt & summon'd them to dance
but they ignor'd my importunate Commotion;
fix'd in ther Places as tho' in a Trance,
staring with painted Eyes at the great Ocean.

VIII

My *Masters* Plan was this: Ther was a Stream
1 hundred Yards or so up-Hill of owr
Camp; in the rainy Season, it became
a raging Torrent, into which we'd lower

owr *Peragua,* as he lik'd to call it;
and let that Torrent bring it down to Sea.
I ask'd him, *How we wou'd ever haul it*
thos hundred Yards? He answer'd, *I wou'd be*

a Beast of Burthen, which do not complayn
no Matter how heavy the Tasks theyr made to do;
he wou'd be likewise, for, Who grutches Pain
that have at last Deliverance in View?

And so we begun. Despite his good Intent
the Labour was inequally divided:
Whenever Shoulders were needed, *Fridays* bent;
whenever Decisions, *Master* decided.

Rollers were cut & lay'd a long the Grownd
a Part of the Way, and the *Canoo* was hoist
upon them: Ropes from her Bow were run a round
a Windlass, which my *Master* had devis'd;

and when we turn'd this Windless, owr *Canoo*
seem'd to a waken; it shudder'd & groan'd
& slid upon thes Rollers for a few
Yards at a Time, till owr Rope was wound

a round the Windlass; or the Rope broke through;
or the Wind-less broke down; or a Roller slid
owt of the Way & stranded the *Canoo*;
or, if som other Thing cou'd fail, it did:

for nothing he ever did was done with Ease
of Natur; for, according to *Providence*,
all Things had Value ownly from ther *Use*,
& had no *Feelings* nor *Intelligence*,

which we call *Spirit*; and which they did withowt;
he call'd me *Savage*, that I cou'd not see
how Things were Tools & how thes Tools allow'd
us to master mor Things: For it appear'd to me

that it was them that master'd us; by making
us work so mutch for What we little needed;
and, when we wanted them, by all Ways breaking;
so that they labour'd rather less than we did.

IX
It took 2 Months befor we reach'd the Stream,
but we were not yet done; *Master* intended,
That the *Canoo* must be slung owt in between
2 opposing Trees, hoist up & suspended

over the Creek, that, once the Flood began
she cou'd be launch'd withowt being swept a Way;
had all Things hapned according to his Plan—
but that they did not, I scarsly need say.

We got the Boat slung in betwixt the Trees
& hoist her up; and then went back to move
owr Camp to the Creek; and then took owr Ease,
he in a Tent & I in the *Canoo,*

which, like a Hammock, lull'd me into Slumber;
I saw my Self (cradl'd in my Dream
by yeelding Flesh, not by unyeelding Timber)
sleeping once mor in my owne Mothers Womb,

as in the Waters under-neath the Earth;
I felt her Body shuddering & trembling
& knew that soon I wou'd be dropp'd in Birth;
and in my Ears hear'd a thund'rous rumbling

which suddenly stopp'd: Now I hear'd someone call
my Name, and sitting up, saw my *Master* drench'd
upon the Bank, poynting to the Wattery Wall
that, at the next Moment, crash'd on me & launch'd

owr *Canoo* onto the swolne River
with me In-side it; tho' not, I fear'd, for long;
as the *Canoo*, a Log once more, roll'd over
& whipp'd a bowt, was taken up & flung

now heer, now ther, now up & now below,
compell'd to dance the Rivers merry Dance;
I griev'd for my *Master*, losing at one Blow
his ownly Servant & his Deliverance,

& shed more Tears for him, than for my Self.
What hapned after this was Wonder-full:
As in my Dream, Wood melted into Flesh
& a warm Hand press'd me to the Hull

a Hull no longer: For the Flood releas'd
the Woman that was hid in the *Canoo*
& with me clinging tightly to her Waist
she swum & frollick'd like a *Whale* or *Sea-Cow*;

I was no longer affraid now of Death,
tho' we dove down Water-Falls immensly high
into the deep Pools that had form'd beneath,
then let the Current take us by & by

the 2 of us at one with the Water
& she cavorting in it merrily
& the arch'd Trees echoing with her Laughter:
As *Dolphins* carry Children, she carry'd me,

my Arms & Legs secure a bowt her fastned:
When she roll'd over on her Belly, I twin'd her
Hair in my Hands

                great Coils of black Hair glisten'd
like *Water-Serpents* streaming owt behind her

X

When *Master* found me at the Streams Embouchure
his Joy in finding that I had not dy'd
seem'd nicely balanc'd by his Discomfiture;
at first kissing & embraceing me, he cry'd

Thou art a live why then I'm not a Loan;
but then his Smiles were driven off by Tears:
O wher has the Hope of my Deliverance gone?
He thwack'd & pummel'd me a bowt the Ears

untill his Arms, exhausted by this Game,
sank to his Sides and he sunk down be Side
me on the Sand wher I'd sank down the same
& then embrac'd me once more & once more cry'd

but beat on me no more. We stay'd like that
for quite a whil, and then he ask'd, *What hapned
to his* Canoo? *Was it stove in or what?*
I told him all that I ha' just now written

except for, What he had all ready seen,
viz, how it broak a Way; but I told him how
it chang'd into the Woman who had been
trapp'd in the Tree, *et cetera*; and how

she carry'd me, once she had gotten owt,
down the whol River, till we came at length
to where he found me, by the Rivers Mouth;
to all of which he listen'd to in Silence,

nodding his Head ownly, a little Bit;
so I went on further, telling him of my
Distress, when I gather'd that she meant to quit
the Island all together, seeing that I

must choose betwicks my *Freedom* & my *Master*,
to whom I ow'd so mutch; here, *Master* nodded:
Lengthening her Stroaks, she swum mutch faster,
heading Sea-ward; till I cry'd owt & prodded

her Flanks with my Toes to-wards the Island;
then she roll'd over on her Back & pick'd me up
& look'd at me for a great long Whil and
smil'd at me, *as at a poor, bedraggl'd Pup,*

for sutch I must ha' seem'd to her no Doubt;
then dropp'd me in be-Side her, and with the
Palm of her Hand, gave me a Push; I struck owt
for the Island, and in a little Whil I'd swum

back to the Rivers Mowth; once safely a Shoar
I try'd to spot her, but she had disappear'd,
and I never saw that Woman any more,
and so I lay down, being suddenly tir'd.

Master say'd nothing, when I was all done,
but meerly sat with his Chin upon his Breast
staring with Eyes vacant of Expression:
When I ask'd him, *If he did not wish to rest,*

he rose & totter'd off on down the Beach;
when he return'd, he had in Hand a few
Peeces of Wood which he had found & which
he say'd was from the broaken-up *Canoo*;

Not possible, says I; but he ignor'd
my owne Account, as, *It did not make Sense:*
Why, no sutch Thing as that never occur'd,
Or wou'd I mock both him & Providence?

XI
At first I little thought how hard my *Master*
took the Loss of owr *Peragua-Canoo*;
but it prov'd, as he say'd, *1 Disaster*
too many for him: That, having gone thro'

sutch a vast Labour of ungrutching Pain
& when Deliverance was near on Hand
to have his bright Hopes extinguish'd by the Rain:
Why, this was too mutch for any Man to stand,

He'd say, shaking his Head in Dis-belief.
And after this, he grew Absent in his Mind,
talking to him-self, mainly, and wandering off
into the Woods with his Jugg of Raisin Wine.

One Evening an Accident occur'd
which left him neer Dead, tho' not entirely:
whil I was cleaning up, he disappear'd,
taking a long his Jugg for Company;

he must ha' wander'd for a good long Time,
pawsing every now & agayn for a Swig;
soon good & lost, he must ha' try'd to climb
a Hill to get his Bearings; but he & the Jugg,

with him half-fill'd & it half-empty, spill'd
down a steep Sloap untill a scrubby Oak
shatter'd the one & very nearly kill'd
the other; inducing in him sutch a Stroak

as left him helpless. When I reach'd him, he
lay withowt moving & ownly roll'd his Eyes
a round his Head as tho' beseeching me
for some Thing or other; but other Wise

he was incapable of Movement or Speech;
I did What little I cou'd do for him
ther & then carry'd him down to the Beach,
& then, the next Day, by easy Stages Home.

Despite my Care for him, he did not regayn
any of thos Powers lost in his Fall;
since Death was certain, I told him of my Plan;
viz., That incertain of *Christian* Buriall,

not having yet been taught by him in this,
but at the same Time, being a *Heathen* no more,
I had som Notions of the Sacrifice
& Ceremony proper to insure

his Souls Release. I thought it for the best
not to belabour this; but meerly to repeat
the Words of his Saviour at the last Feast,
when to his Fellowes, he say'd, *Take ye & eat*

of my owne Flesh in the Remembrance of me;
he seem'd mutch agitated as I spoak
& very pleas'd, as ownly I cou'd see;
but of course, he cou'd say nothing for his Stroak.

XII
Draw a sharp Blade a round the Neck of the Goat
& all 4 Hooves, then make a nother Slyt
with your Knife right at the Base of the Throat
over the Wind-Pipe & then lengthen it,

drawing the Knife down-wards from that Poynt
in a firm Manner, moving down the Breast
& going on untill you come to the Vent;
the Knife Blade shou'd not be too firmly press'd

or the Bagg will rupture, souring the Flesh;
remove the In-sides & scrub owt the Cavity
with Handfulls of twisted Grasses to keep it fresh;
& now the Skin will come off easily,

in 1 single Peece, once the Lymms ha' been slyt
exactly as was mention'd up above;
then work your Blade in betwixt Flesh & Pelt
& peel the latter back-wards like a Glove;

be carefull not to press with the Blade too hard
or you will tear the Pelt; when it's remov'd
use a sharpen'd Shell to scrape a Way the Lard
& Gristle clinging to the In-side; then shave

the Hairs clean off the Out-side; pound to soften
& then stretch it owt to dry in the Sun;
after some Time it will most likely stiffen;
then take it down & pound it once agayn,

softlier this Time; after somemore of this
you will find owt, that in a little While
the Skin of your Goat will mutch resemble his
& may be us'd as Parchment for your Quill.

XIII
Now being my Self entirely a Loan
upon the Island & somewhat at a Loss
for what to do, having so long done
as I was bidden, I waited for his Voice;

and whil I was waiting, I begun to bild
my *Figur Fetisches* a long the Shoar;
and finding that this Occupation fill'd
my Days agreeably, I bilded some more:

When no Ships came, I made up for the Lack
by bilding 1 of Drift-wood Scraps & Peeces;
and, as my Shipps wanted Heathens to attack,
I went to wher the Cannibals had feasted;

tho' not withowt considerable Anxiety;
and after picking Care-fully thro' the Sand
I made some whol *Cannibals* from a Variety
of Parts; taking from this 1 heer a Hand

and from that 1 over ther a broakin Skull
or something els which he no longer needed,
& set them owt to menace my Drift-wood Hull
on Wooden Sticks; after this I added

more Europeans to flesh owt my Crew,
carv'd owt of Wood, with Rifles for Protection;
and then retir'd to admire my *Tableau*,
as tho' I were *God*, after the *Creation:*

How mutch it pleas'd me, to see my Goat Skin Sails
swolne with Breezes; and my Ship lift & plunge
& my brave Crew menac'd by *Cannibals*
& my larger Figurs watching from above;

but after a whil I grew troubl'd in Mind,
& my Heart pounded and I was mutch affraid;
for when I look'd, no wher cou'd I find
no Place for *Friday* in what *Friday* made;

then I was suddenly stricken & the Sun
seem'd to fly In-side my poor bursting Skull
& I stumbl'd dizzily a whil & then
fell down the Way that dead Mens Bodys fall.

XIV
Often in Feaver I wou'd cry owt, dreaming
agayn of my Deliverance: I flee
a Mob of Fiends in humane Bodys screaming
lowder than the Sea-Shoars Foam & Sprye;

I run betwicks the Forest & the Ocean,
but burthen'd with my *Masters* Cloaths & Goods,
fatigu'd & ever slower in my Motion
untill I come by that Poynt in the Woods

from which he lept owt to my Assistance
and pass it by   *nowher is my* Master
no wher Delivery   my ownly Chance
of escaping thes Fiends is to run faster

but tho' I run as tho' my Heart wou'd burst
they gain upon me   ther Cries grow lowder
in my Ears   yet even so I durst
throw no Thing off   Bullets   Baskets   Powder-

Horns   the Muskets which I durst not paws
to load & fire   the Pair of Pumps upon
my Feet   my Chequer'd Shirt   my Linnen Draws
either to fling off all or be undone

and I am seiz'd & flung upon my Back
environ'd by Cannibals that pin me down
whil others of them commence to chop & hack:
the Savage Face I look into is mine

no longer   Why, here I am in Bed, unhurt;
by sputtering Candle, see my wooden Chair;
upon it, folded, see my Draws & Shirt;
and all my Phrenzy vanishes into the Nights Air . . .

Sufficiently recover'd to step owt
the following Morning, I find my Self
puzzl'd, perplex'd, *as in the deepest Doubt*;
standing with my Hand upon the Shelf

next to the Door; upon it, my *Masters* Cloathes
all lay as tho' a waiting his Return
neatly folded. I dress my Self in thes
and take up his Rifle & his Powder-Horn

his Hat & his Umbrella; and so, in his Apparell
I set owt, *as tho' to run a Way from Home*;
what Spirit made me do it, I cannot tell,
nor cou'd I say wher I desir'd to roam,

for it was not I who set owt, nor was it him,
nor was it the both of us to-gether;
I know not who it was; but, as in my Dream
of the Night befor, when I was neither

Master nor *Friday*, but I partook of each,
so it was that Morning. Whatever my Intention
I find my self walking on that Beach
to-wards that Poynt which I have earlier mention'd

and when I pass it by un-harm'd, I collaps
upon the Sand   *I lay ther in great Fear*
for a great long Time   no Savage Shapes
assail mine Eye   no screeching payns mine Ear

CODA: MR DORRINGTON'S DISCOVERY
Ca. 1727

A herd of wild Goats having been reported
we putt 2 Boats a Shoar on an uncharted
Island neer the Mowth of the great River
Oroonoko; and there the Men discover'd
a very agreeable yong Savage,
attir'd in a Suit of Goat Skins.

                           When they enquir'd
merrily, *Was Tayloring his Trade,*
he answer'd them in *English: A Planter made*
this Suit for him & other ones besyde;
but now poor he, that since this Planter dy'd
must be his own Taylor.

                     Ask'd how he came
to dwell here, *Friday* (for that was the Name
this Planter gave him) told the Men this Tale:
That he was rais'd upon a nother Isle
some Ways from heer; and was a Caribb *Prince;*
that he had liv'd on this Isle ever since
captur'd in War-fare by a Tribe that brought him
heer for a Feast; that being what they thought him;
but he escap'd, and liv'd a great long while
with a mis-fortunate Planter from Brazil
who'd run a Grownd here. For nearly 15 Years
(rows of notched shoots became a wall of spears)
until this Planter dy'd, they liv'd together.
This Planter taught him English, et cetera.
This Evening he spoak of unseen Powers
& rav'd, delerious, for severall Howres.
Beside him lay a Goat Skin-Leather Cape

roughly cut into a Mans own Shape.
Earnestly he begg'd me to examine
this Heathen Fetisch; but an inhumane
Stench assail'd me when I try'd to do it,
for a Multitude of Worms had tunnel'd through it,
as Sappers do, to undermine a City
& left it scribbl'd with their rude *Graffiti*.
I ask'd, *Is this your own Divinity?*
All Things do say O to him, was his reply,
and gave it to me, charging me to keep
it for him safely. With that, he fell a Sleep
and I remov'd my Self, taking his Parcell,
which, as I say, reek'd like the very Devill
and was, no Doubt, the Source of his Feaver.
I gave it to my Man to throw it over-
board and now have some Hope he may recover.

VI.
from ROOM FOR ERROR

SHARKS AT THE NEW YORK AQUARIUM

Suddenly drawn through the thick glass plate
And swimming among them, I imagine
Myself as, briefly, part of the pattern
Traced in the water as they circulate
Incessantly obeying the few laws
That thread the needle of their simple lives:
One moment in a cabinet of knives,
Old-fashioned razors and electric saws.
And then the sudden, steep, sidewinding pass:
No sound at all. The waters turning pink,
Then rose, then red, after a long while clear.
And here I am again, outside the tank,
Uneasily wrapped in our atmosphere!
Children almost never tap on the glass.

SNAPSHOT OF DRACULA

Where the face should be, with its thin white lips
Fixed in a smile from which wild honey drips,
There's nothing at all: the mask of assurance slips

From the face of the girl we see up there on the screen
Holding the snapshot carefully between
Two trembling fingers. She stares at the unseen,

The photographic image of non-Being
Beside the image of the image that we're seeing.
For a brief moment, she considers fleeing,

But he's right behind her, just as large as life,
I almost said. And now we hear him laugh:
He too is staring at the photograph,

No doubt amused by this new development.
—How easily her callow and imprudent
Boyfriend, the Doctor from the States, was sent

On a wild goose chase: he will not be back
In time to save her from the Count's attack.
Everything taut now suddenly goes slack:

The Count supports her. So little time to gloat,
So little time to tease that pulsing throat
Before the ending we have learned by rote:

The door flung open, and the poor Count, even
In the moment of his triumph, apprehended,
And the sharp stake driven,
Whuck, whuck, whuck. That Evil may be ended.

SATYR, CUNNILINGUENT: To Herman Melville

1/
Winding her fingers through
His hair, fingertips drumming,
At last she brings him to
The sweet verge of her coming:

Her passion at its flood
Overwhelms all measure;
On articulation's bud,
Inarticulate with pleasure,

She flops like a caught fish,
Straining to be human!
This Satyr has his wish
Fulfilled in a mortal woman.

2/
Flesh is the mystery:
Had Billy a young bride
As Ahab had, would he
Not have been less tongue-tied?

Might he not have become
Glib in the face of darkness
—As you yourself in some
Of your moods seem to practice

The clever, tongue-in-cheek
Art of the cunning Satyr?
How hard it is to speak
Of the things that matter.

WEEKEND *(After Godard)*

"Erotic cannibals, we eat up
Everyone, each other: is *gourmandise*
A verb? Stripping me for form's sake with his eyes,
One index finger stirred a paper cup
Half-full of ice and scotch, we heard the Stones
Make plastic revolution . . . I was bored
With him, with having him as my reward
For clean living: I wanted beads and bones,
Necklaces of chipped teeth . . .

                                  Those nights at your
Place in the Village. I thought of our
One-room fortress falling. History
Is what goes on in spite of us, outside—
Warpainted Mohawks with machine guns glide
By noiselessly, slip from tree to tree . . ."

AFTER

"Nothing happened after. For three days
We waited at the cottage by the lake.
John drove off to town one night for news
And didn't return. I led the children back
Into the woods. I said he'd meet us there.
Worn out too easily, both boys slept
So deeply that I searched their skin and hair . . .
Later, I heard men calling, so I crept
Forward to the cottage . . . sheets of flame
Lay at the window and the open door,
Devouring our summer lives and goods.
I brought the boys back deeper in the woods
And told them we would look next morning for
A new summer place. I said it was a game."

TERMINAL COLLOQUY

O where will you go when the blinding flash
Scatters the seed of a million suns?
And what will you do in the rain of ash?

I'll draw the blinds and pull down the sash,
And hide from the light of so many noons.
But how will it be when the blinding flash

Disturbs your body's close-knit mesh,
Bringing to light your lovely bones?
What will you wear in the rain of ash?

1 will go bare without my flesh,
My vertebrae will click like stones.
Ah. But where will you dance when the blinding flash

Settles the city in a holy hush?
1 will dance alone among the ruins.
Ah. And what will you say to the rain of ash?

I will be charming. My subtle speech
Will weave close turns and counter turns—
No. What will you say to the rain of ash?
Nothing, after the blinding flash.

INSTITUTIONAL LIFE

"Poseidon sat at his desk doing figures. The
administration of the waters gave him endless work."
—Kafka

1/

Doctor, I dream that I am lost and mocked
By hidden voices calling out my name
Behind the doors of houses all the same,
And every door I try is always locked
But one: I open it and walk into
A room in which the hopeless mad are kept . . .
Here no one speaks to me at all, except
For one shy girl who sees that I am new.
"There is a room beyond this one," she says.
"This one is called The Tank, and that's The Pen.
The guards are called The Angels of The Law.
In this room you may do just as you please,
But those who leave here don't come back again."
And then I wake up wondering what I saw.

2/

"Penelope, Telemachos: both gone,
Translated into fiction—you survive,
Barely. If you want to stay alive
You've got to be as quiet as a stone.
This dresser's yours, this is your army cot.
The lunch this afternoon will be fish stew.
They'd want to kill you if they only knew,
They'd want to give you what the others got.
Don't tell them anything."

                              And then she leaves.
Is she the daughter that I never had,
Or the Goddess, always counseling deceit?
I put on one more mask, one more defeat,
A nameless man going slowly mad.
Is it doing, or remembering deceives?

3/
She slips beside me, takes an empty seat,
And smoothes a scrap of paper in her hands:
"Can you make out the writing?" she demands.
The page is blank. She reads me part of it:
"'Beaten by police,' his last notes say,
'For three days running. She would not confess.
M's understanding of the Camps grows less
And less improbable to me each day.
Most likely I will be the next to go;
Begun by chance, it ends of necessity . . .'
That's very old, you know. What's written there.
I took it from a guard who slept with me.
He was tall and slim and had blond hair."
"Why are you back," I ask her.
                              "Don't you know?"

4/

"Believe it but be silent is the way.
Of course you don't remember—it will all
Come slowly back to you: first learn to crawl,
Then learn to walk. Remember that today
Could be the first day of your old, real life.
We must go slowly. There are others who
Are in on it—I've passed the word down to
A friendly guard who knew your son and wife.
In the next few days, a few of us will start
Speaking of it to a few we trust.
We must move slowly, for the walls have ears;
And all the ears have walls. It might take years,
It might not happen ever, but we must
Live our lives as though it will: take heart."

5/

The old connections break, old faces blur,
The greasy skin on a bowl of cold soup . . .
Time's tripped me up, Time's caught me in a loop,
My daily matter. When I think of her
I think of no one: when I think of him,
I see the child I think I used to be;
We renovate the old gags easily,
By switching the direction of the film—
Flapping like wings the dated pages fly
Swarming back onto their calendar;
The custard plastered on the comic's face
Peels off and hurtles backward through the air,
Becoming, instantly, the hefted pie:
Always the audience is pleased by this.

6/

"Returns to find men taking liberties:
The suitors in his place hand him a cup
Of wine, some meat. The suitors have made up
Stories of how King Odysseus
Returns to find men taking liberties,
The suitors in his place. Gladly they tell
How King Odysseus sent them to hell!
They tell him that a guest should wish to please,
They say, 'It's a wise beggar entertains.'
He rises slowly, winish, tottering:
Telling his story would be suicide.
He makes up an excuse and steps outside.
Begins to run. At his back the devouring
Legend follows, anxious for remains . . ."

7/

Every night we heard their senseless cries
Rise up and mingle in the hot air—
The wall between us sagged, dripping with their
Sweat, or billowed out to ecstacies,
Aching like a membrane, paper thin—
Her double, her double's foreign lover, who
Lay in there so closely that they knew
The walls around them as their only skin....
They beat like moths against the one wall they
Shared with us, it was another world—
We listened for them, nights. Dying, they broke
Open like bread, their fractioned bodies spoke,
While we lay apart and tightly curled
In the damp palm of what we could not say.

8/

All things are possible: the man I was
Or may have been was many men besides
And many beasts, all chained up as the tides
Are, all fiercely roaring as the wind does.
That was what the goddess Kirke knew,
My witching pedagogue. She taught me well:
"What follows function?"

          "Form does."

                    "That's the spell:
Each of your crewmen was a human zoo."
Embrace a goddess, penetrate her charms:
Simple as that. I might have gone to bed
With Kirke, studied magic in her arms:
"So many murders, armed robberies, and rapes—
Your men *were* swine," Kirke might have said.
"Little labor, finding their true shapes."

9/

He had no stories, feeding on the raw
Meat of experience, then voiding it:
The past was excrement to his small wit,
The future flesh to cram into his maw.
He narrowed my few options down to one:
"A good wine, but it doesn't travel well . . .
We left Poseidon's pinhead in his cell
Snoring and bubbling: he'd had his fun
And we'd had ours. Each night in his dreams
I am the clumsy self-pitying child,
He is the hero who can never lose.
And for an instant in his sleep we fuse
Together, one, before he leaps up wild
With pain, the steep cave cracking to his screams.

10/

Assurances accept me: I fit in,
I take a part in things for my own good:
Last week I carved some figures out of wood.
All I have to do is toe the line
And keep my eye out for the basic flaw:
It's easy time. I almost like the life.
The other day I made myself a knife
Out of scraps, today I used the power saw . . .
I see my enemies, their faces turn
Into the masks of bats flying to hell,
Slaughtered for their indolence and greed!
They tell me, "Work, keep busy, you'll get well . . .
I'm older now and slower—what I need
To know takes me much longer now to learn.

11/

My name, repeated: her insistent shout
Is shattered by long laughter in the trees.
In my dream I mumble Dear God please
Let her find me this time let her lead me out.
Doctor, I've had this dream now for a week,
Always the same wilderness, the same
Long laughter shattering the shouted name.
She calls and calls me but I cannot speak.
What maid is this who does not fear the lion's
Eye and tangled mane and nakedness?
What god or goddess urges her to bring
Him from the bleak shore of that wilderness
To the city of her father, the mild king
Of the blameless and essential Phaiakians?

12/

Her disappearance: elegant, almost
Flamboyant: grand! She's on the outside now,
I'm sure of it although I'm not sure how.
Vanished just like Hamlet's father's ghost.
The guards all tell me that she was removed:
"A troublemaker, not at all like you;
It wasn't nice, but what else could we do?
We asked permission and Himself approved."
I think this alters my uncertain role;
Maybe it's time for me to disappear,
Maybe I'll do it now.

                          This afternoon.

                                 Tonight.

I'll vanish down my rabbit hole
And then come back to haunt them:

                        KNOCK KNOCK

                               "Who's there?"

A secret smile before I answer, "No one."

HEROIC ATTITUDES

I

He has always feared the awakening dead,
Has offered his flesh to feed their hunger
When they rose in the darkness around his bed.
He has always feared their lordly anger.

This was their song: "An endless river,
Flowing in silence, carries us on
Through every weather. The past is the lover
You hold in your arms, going and gone."

He remembers the painful death of his father,
And often at night remembers the son
Set out to die in terrible weather.
His horse stumbles on a sharp stone.

He cannot escape to a different weather,
A place out of reach of the lordly dead.
Every night he must watch them gather
In a bright ring around his bed.

Today he rides through a distant wood
To answer a question or question an answer
Which once he thought he understood.
The black trees sway with the weight of their branches.

His wife, the Queen, turns from her mirror:
Below, in the courtyard, a riderless horse
Gallops in circles, plunging with terror,
Returned from where the three roads cross.

II
His wife, the Queen, turns from her mirror
The wind in the forest is combing its leaves
She combs her hair, which tumbles like fire
The wind in the forest quietly weaves
A chamber of silence over the King
Until his life is no more than a rumor
Covered by leaves that are withering
The lips of the King are twisting, not terror

Presses his mouth, not the mouth of a lover
But some indescribably slower thing
Winds through him like a meandering river
The plains of his flesh are rippling
When the rippling stops he will turn into stone
And the leaves will press dry fingers over
Lamentation of flesh, sorrow of bone
She sees it as in a dream, in a fever

And cries out aloud, shaking with terror
And the birds rise screaming and are gone
All taking flight from a single tremor
They have left her there in the forest alone
She combs out her hair in the forest a tree
Combs out its leaves, which tumble like fire
Burning to ashes her husband's body
And she sits in silence before her mirror

III

He wonders now, if, having so far defied
Whatever it was that told him clearly, "No!"
He may leave his sleeping, ambiguous bride;
Or, if he chooses instead not to go,

Will he be forced later to put on
A foolish mask, pretending ignorance
Of what he is and what it is he has done?
And while assorted figures do their dance

Of discovery, dredge up forgotten clues,
Come in with the truth wriggling on their hooks,
Must he pretend amazement at the maze?
—Guessing by their careless, smirking looks

That they have always known what now appears,
Monstrous, cold, slimy with afterbirth . . .
Might he perhaps live on, unknown for years,
Until all who know are folded in the earth?

There is still time to leave before she wakes,
Rolling from sleep unsated, full of lust—
Pull down the shades, muffle all the clocks,
Slip out at dawn like her true husband's ghost—

There is no way to leave before her death,
For where would he go, and how could he be free?
The prize he won is ashes in his mouth,
But life here has a pleasing symmetry.

FOUR FOR THEODORE ROETHKE

I. The Circle
Out of the matrix of all metaphor
Resemblance came: one feather was a wing,
One wing a bird, circling before
The shaded absences of everything.
And when all birds were flown, his mind could seize
On the vibrating emptiness of trees,

Could make a song of what was almost there,
Tilting into what was nearly gone.
He loved the edges, where the changes are;
In a still place, he clattered like a stone
On the far side of things; the mirror's kiss,
A mountain nibbled on by its abyss,

The silence that surrounded every word,
Sheathlike, flamelike, quivering to sound—
It was in darkness he most clearly heard
The smallest cry out of the brewing ground,
The meanest voice, cracking like a whip.
He measured out the snail's becoming step,

Danced with bears, edged toward openings;
Standing at the center of his field
He brought us news of all insensible things,
The near, deep lives of another world:
Nudged by beginnings, echoes drew him out;
Inevitable endings cut him short.

II. The Garden
In the ruined kingdom of his father's house
There were no secrets, all the outside
Leaned like a lover on its fragile glass;
A bridegroom pressing a resistant bride
Would not lean heavier. He held his breath
And counted slowly; after ten came death.

But in the canceled greenhouse of his memory
When it was summer throughout all the year,
The vast, unmeasured outside let him be,
And even death backed down, speechless before
The iron mandate of his father's will.
He came back often to that citadel

Which looked to him as to an only child,
And stood in the fierce lightnings of his father's eye,
In the beauty and horror of a world
Where flowers tumbled from an old man's thigh,
All falling into light at his command—
In the upraised province of his father's hand

He cast no stones: waited, biding time;
Beyond the narrow garden was a field
And in that field the shadow of a rhyme
Fell across occasions which revealed
A world of endless, varied sequence; he
Bent to it, like a lover, secretly.

III. The Dance
All history was troubled by a dream,
The constant world shook with metaphor.
In an open field once before their time
He summoned her as water, aether, air—
Wishing was having then, and branch was root—
They flourished like the dead do, underfoot

(The dead have no perspective on events),
They came together there, they broke apart,
Were fiery as grass beneath a lens
And like the fishes in the water, wet.
He knew her body's risk, his body's task;
Wild speech took shape behind a formal mask,

Passion was measured in a patterned dance,
A dance the dead do, all out of place
(The easy dead are anywhere at once);
He taught her words she knew, and he learned grace.
Each hung in silence on the other's lips:
Dead children quivered at their fingertips,

Rippling like rumors through a long embrace,
Or bent back steeply like a candle flame
To feed in whispers on an empty face—
In that fond dancing each of them became
The other's answer to the asking dead.
—How one would follow where the other led!

IV. The Burden
The burden flowering at heavy cost:
He knew the cost, knew how the burgeoning
Bough shudders in the wind, already lost—
And the heavy price paid when the opening
Buds become the blossoms on a tree;
Those blossoms ripen and they break their bough.

No longer pacing out his middle age,
He tumbled quickly to an ecstacy,
He loosened into love, that purest rage,
Impossible to risk or justify:
Circumference was never more than here
And now, no end was on it, anywhere—

There was no edge, there was no edge at all!
He knew the virtue of some secret name,
It was impossible for him to fall:
Bobbing like a blossom on a stem
He was indifferent to all but joy,
And with his words he gave himself away:

Inside the cherry is the lightest stone,
But nonetheless the cherry's branches cry
Out at its weight: they cannot bear for long
The burden of their joy. No more could he.
That heavy body bore a glistening word.
Now fold his hands away, misunderstood.

PROPOSAL FOR A MONUMENT OF PEARS

Four pears in all, and all of them gigantic:
Two in the foreground, looming up, obscurely
Questioning our values, giving answers
In an ambiguous fashion, which will surely
Offer much comfort, solace: the distressed of
Heart will remain here in grey droves for hours,
Until the last pear seems to them the breast of
A green girl, ripening. Beyond it towers
The patriarch of pears—orgulous, sullen,
Not to be sliced compliantly in wedges
And taken as dessert with runny cheeses.
Restored, the pilgrims sink upon their knees as
They see the carved words, brown around the edges,
Of its simple inscription: *FOR THE FALLEN*

LOVE IN THE CITY OF REFLECTED LIGHT

Being deceives, they believe: their existence
Depends on hours spent in front of the mirrors
Surrounding them. They watch as their reflections
Undress, dress and undress; they finger themselves
Coyly, with what they think of as abandon:
Though there is no one there who doesn't notice,

It is considered impolite to notice,
At least in public places, the existence
Of habits some deplore but none abandon;
No matter how far removed they are from mirrors
They must inevitably find themselves
As much involved with them as those reflections

Which are the subject of their best reflections:
"And how long will it be before they notice
That we can love only the images themselves,
And by so doing, have given them existence,
Have made them independent of the mirrors
Which they will certainly, in time, abandon?

"Were we to go so far as to abandon
This city which we love to its reflections,
Or forge a great hammer and shatter all the mirrors,
Those saucy images would not take notice;
How long before they question our existence?"
And even as the speakers reveal themselves

In troubled words, the very words themselves
Betray their speakers, rapidly abandon
Meaning and motive both: fade from existence
Like lovers stripped before their own reflections,
To echo in infinity unnoticed.
"Mere words," their saying goes, "will fog no mirrors."

That city, so unlike ours, strangely mirrors
Ours in some ways—ways which in themselves
May not matter. But of course you will notice
An explanation much too neat to abandon:
The people of that city are our reflections.
They say that it will pass out of existence

When the mirrors waken to their own existence:
Conscious of themselves, they will, without notice
Shatter, abandoning their lost reflections.

CALVUS IN RUINS

I

verbosa gaudet Venus loquella

Venus loves nothing more than juicy gossip,
lewd & lascivious badinage, highly
spiced with erotic words whose double meanings
    have double meanings:

that is what pleases her. And when she gets it,
swiftly her tongue insinuates its clever
tip into pauses in the conversation,
    exciting Rumor,

who flutters off in eighty-two directions
spreading all sorts of havoc   *   *
*   *   *   *   *   *
    even great cities.

Therefore be careful if you have a secret
lover with whom you make love in great peril
of discovery: those sweet times are precious
    which you have stolen,

and only silence will allow you hours
more of such riches: words will never buy them,
words will only bring that mischief which Venus
    loves nothing more than.

II

*   *   *   *   *   my

delicate songs are popular at parties,

my   *   *   *   *   *

    have been collected;

yet he is certainly to be more envied
who may embrace you whenever he wishes,
even while I must lurk under your window,
    suffering bitter-

ly from chills & debilitating fevers,
which take their turns at racking my small body
until I stagger off in utter torment,
    mocked by street urchins!

But these are trifles, which I mention only
to make this song of mine for your amusement
*   *   *   *   *   *

    if you would have me

while I am still sufficient to those pleasures
we shared together, when, in someone else's
*   *   *   *   *   *

    send me a few words.

III
*   *   *   *   *   *
*   *   *   *   *   *
*   *   *   *   *   *

    Caesar & Pompey:

one word from either, and whole armies perish
*   *   *   *   *   *
provinces catch fire, distant   *   *
    illuminated;

*   *   *   *   *   *

but what I've written will endure forever,
*   *   *   *   *   *

    strewn with blank corpses.

IV
Whatever is likeliest to happen, does:
the maiden in the orchard is deflowered;
the drunken husband, home from brothel-hopping,
    finds his wife in bed

with Caesar & a few of Caesar's cronies;
some sickening old fool is given poison
by his young wife, unfettered as the weary
    day turns into night;

the marble children Praxiteles sired,
dismembered limb by limb, are   *
*   *   parchment flares at the edges,
    then bursts into flame!

But in the distant provinces, decaying
corpses get up & trundle off to market
places already agog with the rumor
    of yet another

two-headed chicken, another virgin birth.
There, it would seem, all seeing is deceiving;
nothing is said that doesn't find believers;
    they fancy poets.

V
    (a)
Withering laurel: in his old age, Caesar
will have forgotten all of the costly gains
on British battlefields, in Roman bedrooms;
    sieges & conquests

which are now brilliant in his eyes will perish
*   *   *   *   *   *
these ruined cities or those ruined women,
    equally nameless.

Soon no one living will remember Caesar,
but memory itself will be forgotten
before your name is   *   *   *
    your slightest gesture;

*   *   *   *   *   *
*   *   like the crumbs of flowers
on a madman's chin   *   *   *
    *   *   *

(b)

Memory draws my bowstring, and the arrow
trembles a moment   *   *   *
*   *   *   indifferent to fame
　　as any poet!

VI

　　　　　　　　　　a virgo infelix, herbis pasceris amaris
*   *   *   *   *   *
*   *   *   *   *   *

boredom's a bitter stalk for you to nibble,
　　unlucky virgin;

outside the city everything is boring,
life is a nuisance   *   *   *
and Venus is indeed the most important
　　goddess in heaven;

I'm sympathetic, I agree completely;
but even the sun that journeys endlessly
has sense enough to rest when near exhaustion:
　　can't you do likewise?

VII

　　(a)

Before your restless ashes had been sifted
the quick connective tissue of your poems
already had begun a slower burning;
　　now next to nothing,

what little bits of you were spared for reading
hardly make sense—the dreck that critics salvaged
simply to score a point or two on usage,
    *   *   *

    (b)
Once my rhetoric defeated Cicero's,
my eloquence made Vatinius sputter,
"Must I be hanged because this shrimp can whistle?"
    That doesn't matter:

whatever we have made well will at last come
to utter nothing in the house of Orcus,
*   *   *   *   *   *
    *   *   *

VIII
Think of Achilles, maddened by his hatred,
leaping from one wet stone onto another,
pursuing those who are already shadows
    as he heads upstream,

an unrelenting fury in that river
where the cold-eyed fish tumbled in its currents
are delicately stripping bloated corpses
    of their fat cargo;

or think of women delicately weaving
patterns as subtle as the webs of spiders
*   *   *   *   *   *
    *   *   *

stained with human blood; think of two great armies
coming together on a dusty field: when all the tumult ends,
there are some men who clatter off rejoicing,
        and others who stay;

these are all noble subjects for reflection,
but when you read my book, think of making love
late in the morning to a supple woman
        on a narrow bed.

IX

*   *   *   *   *   *
*   *   *   *   *   *
*   *   *   *   *   *

        wretched without you.

Oh, I exaggerate. Exaggeration
flutters, poor timid gelding! understatement
roars like a lion—and that imposing team
        draws my chariot

around the track unevenly   *   *
*   *   *   *   I wobble
*   *   *   *   *   *

        mistress of revels!

X

Another man, another woman lying

*   *   *   *   *   *

*   *   if it is my pleasure

    simply to watch you

*   *   *   *   *   *

*   *   and the laughter surrounding

the edges of our conversation,

    which silence devours.

XI

    (a)

but *you* will not escape from my embraces

    (b)

*   *   *   *   *   *

*   *   *   *   *   *

this also pleases her, delights the golden

    Venus of Eryx.

Note: Gaius Licinius Macer Calvus, 82–47 B.C. One of the closest friends of Catullus, "he was renowned as a most able and skillful orator, though of low stature, and as a writer of epic, lyric, and epigram." (E. T. Merrill) Only a few fragments of his verse survive.

TAKEN UP

Tired of earth, they dwindled on their hill,
Watching and waiting in the moonlight until
The aspens' leaves quite suddenly grew still,

No longer quaking as the disc descended,
That glowing wheel of lights whose coming ended
All waiting and watching. When it landed

The ones within it one by one came forth,
Stalking out awkwardly upon the earth,
And those who watched them were confirmed in faith:

Mysterious voyagers from outer space,
Attenuated, golden—shreds of lace
Spun into seeds of the sunflower's spinning face—

Light was their speech, spanning mind to mind:
We come here not believing what we find—
Can it be your desire to leave behind

The earth, which even those called angels bless,
Exchanging amplitude for emptiness?
And in a single voice they answered *Yes,*

Discord of human melodies all blent
To the unearthly harmony of their assent.
Come then, the Strangers said, and those who were taken, went.